Alvaro Martins

The Role of Computerisation in Brazilian Small and Medium-sized Enterprises

Alvaro Martins

The Role of Computerisation in Brazilian Small and Medium-sized Enterprises

Digital Transformation - How to get started?

ScienciaScripts

Imprint

Cover image: www.ingimage.com

This book is a translation from the original published under ISBN 978-613-9-69885-1.

Publisher:
Sciencia Scripts
is a trademark of
Dodo Books Indian Ocean Ltd. and OmniScriptum S.R.L publishing group

120 High Road, East Finchley, London, N2 9ED, United Kingdom
Str. Armeneasca 28/1, office 1, Chisinau MD-2012, Republic of Moldova, Europe
Printed at: see last page
ISBN: 978-620-8-14260-5

I dedicate this thesis to my wife Patrícia and my daughter Isabella, with whom I have had the privilege of living and sharing love, dreams, hopes and joys.

ACKNOWLEDGEMENTS

I thank the good Lord who has always blessed me with good health and lots of energy.

I would like to thank my father, Carlos Henrique, and my mother, Silbeni, for their love, support and encouragement, which have always been and continue to be decisive in my formation and journey so far.

I would like to thank my beloved wife Patrícia, who has lovingly provided me with affection, understanding and tolerance during these years of struggle and the search for new ideals.

I would like to thank my beloved daughter Isabella, who has brought so much light into my life, making our life full of joy, being my greatest inspiration and source of energy.

I would like to thank Prof Dr Fernando de Souza Meirelles, my advisor, role model and reference, who with his wisdom has inspired and guided me from the beginning of this demanding doctoral period to the conclusion of this work, knowing how to charge and also encourage.

I would like to thank Prof Dr Alberto Luiz Albertin, who has accompanied me since the early days of my postgraduate studies at this school, always showing me the way and supporting me, as well as sharing valuable academic teachings.

I would like to thank the professors and fellow PhD students for the moments we shared and for how much they taught me during these intense and enjoyable years together.

I would like to thank all those who, directly or indirectly, helped me to complete this important stage in my life.

"A vision without action is just a dream.
Action without vision is just a pastime.
But a vision with action can change the world".

Joel Barker

SUMMARY

In today's environment of globalised competition, there is growing recognition of the central role of Information Technology (IT) in determining a company's success and leading it to better results.
Small and medium-sized companies also adopt IT with the same aim of obtaining benefits from its use, but their reality is, in most cases, quite different from that of large companies, especially as they don't have the same resources and skills in the IT area. In addition to competition, sometimes other factors, such as legal requirements in the Brazilian case, force companies to seek greater computerisation.
As companies are at different stages in terms of computerisation, especially the role that IT plays for each one, the aim of this thesis is to see if there is an association between IT spending and investment and the performance of small and medium-sized Brazilian companies.
The study seeks to capture the differences in the company's results resulting from the use of IT. To this end, it looks at financial data, also taking into account executives' perceptions of the stages of computerisation and the role that IT plays in the company.
The methodology adopted involved the application of questionnaires to obtain quantitative data on the profile of IT use and financial information, as well as qualitative data on the perception of the role IT plays in companies.
The cluster analysis technique was then applied, which showed four groupings with different behaviours in relation to the variables, called "Digital"; "Prudent"; "Conservative" and "Analogue".
The results found point to evidence of the relationship between IT spending and investment and increased company profitability, especially given the presence of specific perceptions among managers about the role IT plays in the company.
Companies that have a higher level of IT spending and investment, coupled with a strong perception on the part of managers that IT can contribute positively to the company's objectives, result in a higher level of profitability; while companies whose managers strongly perceive that IT cannot contribute positively to the company's objectives, even if they make levels considered to be above average IT spending and investment, have a lower level of profitability.
355 small and medium-sized Brazilian companies were studied, and the main conclusion was that the greater the managers' perception of the positive impact of IT on the company's business processes as a whole, the greater the impact of IT spending and investment on the company's profitability.

Keywords: Information technology and competitiveness. Small and medium-sized enterprises (SMEs). Perceptions about stages of computerisation and the role of IT. IT performance and effectiveness.

SUMMARY

CHAPTER 1

Introduction

A company's ultimate goal is to achieve perennial profit and, to this end, it endeavours to make the best possible use of its resources, allocating them according to the business strategies it has drawn up, in order to be competitive. Many theories show this (Hamel and Prahalad, 1996; Lemos et al. 2011; Yen-Tsang, Csillag and Siegler, 2012).

More recently, and increasingly, we have seen technology play an important role in companies, making it one of the most important resources in the pursuit of any company's ultimate goal, as mentioned in Moraes, Cappellozza and Meirelles (2011).

As we can see from various studies (Bhatt and Grover, 2005; Tallon and Kraemer, 2007; Nevo, Wade and Cook, 2010, Higon, 2011, Ollo-Lopez and Aramendia-Muneta, 2012), technology has always been a central variable in organisational theory, and its use by companies has intensified, as shown by the ever-increasing spending. In Brazil, total annual IT spending and investment by companies, when measured as a percentage of revenue, grew at an average rate of 7.6 per cent per year from 1988 to 2014 (Meirelles, 2015).

Another central question regarding the use of IT by companies is whether this practice leads to improved performance, a topic that has already been studied by several authors (Melville, Kraemer and Gurbaxani, 2004; Lozinsky, 2008; Cao, 2010), but with controversial results, since some studies point to positive results, while others say that there is no relationship, or even that the results are negative, and there is room for greater understanding.

According to Orlikowski (2000), both organisations and technology have undergone dramatic changes in format and function and, consequently, changes in management and evaluation are also imperative.

This view is also shared by Nolan and Mc Farlan (2005), for whom the dizzying pace of change in the world of technology and the changes that IT can bring to the business elevate IT issues to a high level of importance.

In the same vein, Albertin (2010) shows us that, in this new reality, organisations have become virtual in a totally interconnected environment, which has required significant changes in organisational guidelines, including their structure and rules of authority and responsibility.

According to Yoo (2010), the changes are so profound in the use of IT by companies and people (making the concept of ubiquitous computing a reality today) that even the study of the area should take this into account, expanding the scope of research.

Weill, Woerner and Mocker (2014) add that in this current stage of computerisation, in which we see many companies living in an environment they call "total digitalisation", the challenges for high-performance management are enormous.

An even greater complexity is found when analysing small and medium-sized enterprises (SMEs), which, despite playing an important role in economic and social development worldwide, cannot be viewed through the same lens as large companies (Devos, Landeghem and Deschoolmeester, 2012).

Based on these changes and a number of factors, such as the growing digital business environment, we can see the role of politicians and governments creating laws that oblige small businesses to become computerised, and technology suppliers increasingly seeing small and medium-sized businesses as potential customers. We also found a number of academic studies aimed at better understanding the issue in small and medium-sized businesses (Dierckx and Stroeken, 1999; Southern and Tilley, 2000; Haug, Pedersen and Arlbjorn, 2011).

In Brazil, there have also been some studies into the impact of technology use by small and medium-sized Brazilian companies, such as Gonçalves (1994), who studied the services sector, Prates and Ospina (2004), who looked at various sectors, and Lunardi, Dolci and Maçada (2010), who also showed the relationship between IT adoption and its impact on perceived organisational performance.

Still on the subject of the role of governments in the degree of computerisation of companies, when it comes to emerging economies like Brazil, there seems to be a strong influence on the process of diffusion of innovations, as described by Diniz, Rodrigues and Ferrer (2007). We also want to analyse this through the obligation imposed by the Brazilian government for companies to present their tax information digitally, according to Decree 6.022 of 22/01/2007.

According to data from SEBRAE - Serviço Brasileiro de Apoio às Micros e Pequenas Empresas (2014), the rate of entrepreneurship in Brazil has increased consistently compared to other countries. In 2013, there were more than 21 million Brazilians in charge of entrepreneurial activities, which means small and medium-sized businesses.

This research aims to contribute to the growing field of study of the use of technology by small and medium-sized enterprises and to observe how this can affect their performance and consequent competitiveness.

In the structure of this work, we first find the description of objectives, in which we seek to present the problem in question with the respective objectives; then we present a part that aims to clarify the justifications for this thesis; then we move on to the theoretical framework of the subject, describing what has already been said about IT and competitiveness; the work addresses and describes the main contributions on the issue of performance and effectiveness of IT spending and investment, which has several nuances and possibilities of understanding, especially in small and medium-sized enterprises (SMEs), which is another topic addressed in depth. The theoretical framework concludes with an understanding of what has already been written about the perception of the stages of computerisation and the role of IT in the company.

The next chapter aims to present the theoretical framework of what will be covered in this work and is divided into five parts: in the introduction, we first seek to contextualise the subject; then address the topic of IT and competitiveness; describe the main contributions already known on the issue of performance and effectiveness of IT spending and investment; then conceptualise small and medium-sized enterprises - SMEs; and finally propose a model to analyse how IT spending and investment can influence performance, mediated by the perception of the stages of computerisation and the role of IT in the company.

CHAPTER 2

Research problem

The results presented each year by the companies that make up the Information Technology market demonstrate the great competence that these companies have to produce and sell, but the question that appears relevant is whether this growing use of technology brings benefits to companies. And for small Brazilian companies in particular, does this use bring results in terms of their competitiveness?

Several studies have shown that the most important thing is not simply to acquire the technology, looking at it as an end in itself in order to obtain the expected results. In order to extract any benefit from technology, its use must be borne in mind, thinking of technology as a means to achieve specific objectives (Maçada, Becker and Lunardi, 2005; Albertin and Albertin, 2012; Laudon and Laudon, 2013). With regard to the search for constant profit in every company, the work of Longo and Meirelles (2015) makes an important contribution, researching large Brazilian industries, and shows that for every 1% of spending and investment made in IT, a 7.3% increase in operating profit was found.

The literature review found that the majority of existing studies deal with medium-sized and large companies, as small businesses have very different conditions (Arendt, 2008; Steinfield et al., 2012; Piget and Kossai, 2013). This study seeks to explore the issue further in this context.

Some studies show that the results of the use of Information Technology in companies can be influenced by the maturity of the company (Nolan, 1979), as well as the role that IT plays in the company (McFarlan, 1984).

However, there are numerous factors that can impact the company's result, as well as numerous factors specific to the use of IT that can also impact the result. So, are maturity and role specific factors that explain this result? How? Are higher levels of maturity able to extract better benefits from the use of IT and consequently better results? Can different views on the role of IT in the company lead to different benefits and results from the use of IT?

Given the increasingly important role that Information Technology is playing in the organisational scenario, a fact also proven by the growing expenditure, this research seeks to answer the following question:

What is the impact of IT spending and investment on the financial performance of small and medium-sized Brazilian companies?

To answer this question, the work also addresses the following aspects:

- executives' perception of the stages of computerisation and the role IT plays in the company, showing different possibilities and seeking to verify whether these differences have an impact on performance;

- conversion or effectiveness of IT by conceptualising the improvement of organisational performance.

2.1 Objectives

2.1.1. General

To see if there is an association between IT spending and investment and the performance of small and medium-sized enterprises, and also to measure managers' perceptions of the stages of computerisation and the role that IT plays in the company.

2.1.2. Specific

To map , among small and medium-sized national companies, clusters of companies according to managers' perceptions of the stages of computerisation and the role that IT plays in the company, in order to clarify whether there is any distinct pattern of behaviour, by clusters, of IT spending and investment and financial performance for the sample studied;

-Identify the relationship between IT spending and investment and Net Annual Profit over the period studied.

2.2 Justification

This thesis is justified because, as far as can be seen from the literature review, there is no news of studies showing the possible relationship between IT spending and investment and the performance of small and medium-sized Brazilian companies, also mediated by managers' perceptions of the role IT plays in the company and the stages of computerisation.

In addition, many studies found in the literature on the subject point to the difficulty of predicting the results of IT spending and investment (Dewan, Shi and Gurbaxani, 2007; Dewan and Ren, 2011; Otim et al., 2012), which should not affect the responsibility of managers to ensure the broad and effective use of IT, as shown by several other studies (Remenyi, 2000; Weill and Ross, 2004; Flyvbjerg and Budzier, 2011).

This thesis is also justified because it could contribute both to understanding the elements that lead to performance through IT spending and investment in small and medium-sized Brazilian companies, and to managers of these types of companies analysing and making better decisions about the use of IT.

In the highly competitive scenario in which most companies find themselves today, where the computerisation of society has reached high levels, it is essential that companies are able to extract the best benefits from IT spending and investment, which will be addressed in this research.

Another relevant aspect is the evaluation of IT spending and investments and their impact on company performance, also known as IT effectiveness, as there is a lot of discussion in the literature, including a great deal of disagreement, indicating the need for further discussion in this regard (Hitt and Brynjolfsson, 1996; Kohli and Devaraj, 2003; Maçada, Becker and Lunardi, 2005; Mithas et al., 2012).

This thesis seeks to contribute to the discussion, particularly in the Brazilian context, by focusing on financial performance, especially in small and medium-sized companies.

Due both to the impact that the constant and accelerated changes in the environment have on organisations and society and to the evolution of technology itself, companies have increasingly opted for greater spending and investment in IT, and this topic has become increasingly important in the corporate context. This research will cover the subject in sufficient depth to better understand it from a scientific point of view.

CHAPTER 3

Theoretical foundation

3.1. Information technology and competitiveness

The concept of Information Technology is broader than that of data processing, information systems, software engineering, computing or hardware and software, as it also involves human, administrative and organisational aspects (Keen, 1993).

As in the view of Henderson and Venkatraman (1993), for us the term Information Technology covers the technical aspects, including information systems, the use of hardware and software, telecommunications, automation, multimedia resources, used by organisations to provide data, information and knowledge (Weill, 1992; Luftman and Brier, 1999), as well as issues relating to the workflow, people and information involved.

IT has evolved from a traditional administrative support orientation to a strategic role within the organisation. We can see the evolution of the importance of IT by looking at the accelerated development of the use of this technology in companies. As Meirelles (2015) shows us, "more than 50% of the total capital investments made by American companies have been in IT; in large Brazilian companies, it is estimated that this figure is above 45% and rising".

Several studies have pointed to the link between IT and competitiveness, which has become much more intense since the mid-1990s and is one of the most important driving forces for business in the 21st century, making it vitally important for managers and academics to understand the transformative power of IT and its potential impact on business (Agarwal and Lucas, 2005; McAfee and Brynjolfsson, 2008; Govindarajan and Trimble, 2011).

As we can see from analysing various studies (Jeffrey and Leliveld, 2004; Lunardi, Becker and Maçada, 2012; Laudon and Laudon, 2013), in order to obtain benefits that lead to greater competitiveness, it is not enough simply to acquire IT, but above all to make good use of it, both internally and in relationships with other companies, which can result in the creation of value for the company (Melville, Kraemer and Gurbaxani, 2004; Melville, Gurbaxani and Kraemer, 2007; Albertin and Albertin, 2012).

According to Mata, Fuerst and Barney (1995), although the concept that IT is a powerful competitive weapon is widely emphasised, the sustainability of this competitive advantage is not always well explained. The authors developed a model to analyse the issue and concluded that the only thing that sustains this competitive advantage is competence in IT management.

By combining arguments from the resource-based view theory with the theory of command and control in organisations, the authors Ravichandran et al. (2009) carried out research with US industries and also came to the conclusion that investments in IT contribute to better company performance.

Also contributing to a better understanding, Lin (2007) carried out an interesting study of 155 banks, in which he showed that IT capacity in the companies studied implied value creation and better performance; in other words, the author shows that IT capacity can be an important tool for creating economic value.

Various studies have shown that the benefits of using IT can be measured both tangibly and intangibly, using the impact on the company's financial results, as well as the impact on improving business performance, measured through cost reductions, increased productivity and greater flexibility (Hitt and Brynjolfsson, 1996; Melville; Kraemer and Gurbaxani, 2004; Devaraj and Kohli, 2003; Aral and Weill, 2007).

Since we are interested in the organisational level of analysis in our study, we will focus on the dimensions of IT use related to the following benefits: costs, productivity and innovation (Albertin, 2009).

On the other hand, there are also studies that question whether IT has the ability to create value for the company, as the authors Mooney, Gurbaxani and Kraemer show us in their work

(1996), who claim that there is little evidence that this value creation exists. However, the authors also question the approaches that have been taken to study this relationship, going so far as to propose a new approach to conceptualising the impact of IT on company value, which they say offers a new perspective and a practical guide to assessing the creation of company business value.

Other studies also point out the risk of IT investments, which can vary greatly and sometimes even jeopardise business continuity, especially in small and medium-sized companies that don't have the same resources as large companies (Remenyi, Griffiths and Diniz, 2004; Flyvbjerg and Budzier, 2011; Lunardi, Becker, Maçada, 2012).

The relationship between Information Technology and competitiveness has long been a source of much discussion, with claims that companies spend a lot of money on IT but don't get a reasonable return on these investments, such as the so-called "IT Productivity Paradox", which states that "the computer age can be seen everywhere but in productivity statistics" (Wolff, 1999; Triplett, 1999; Gordon, 2001). Other studies, such as those by Brynjolfsson and Hitt (1995, 1996, 1998, 2000); Brynjolfsson and Yng (1996) and Lichtenberg (1995), have found strong evidence that IT investments can yield substantial returns, refuting the productivity paradox.

In this context of uncertainty, issues such as "risk of failure", "potential for business transformation", "complexity of measuring returns", "control of results", all of which are addressed by IT Governance, are becoming increasingly relevant, especially in terms of understanding how to effectively turn IT spending and investment into business benefits (Weill and Ross, 2004; Weill and Ross, 2006; De Haes and Grembergen, 2009).

Since there is no consensus on the impact of IT on the company, we have tried in this research to contribute to a better understanding of the subject, especially in the case of small and medium-sized Brazilian companies.

3.2 IT performance and effectiveness

Although performance is a key concept in various theoretical perspectives such as the resource-based view or team management, and is even used in various academic studies, in reality there is no consensus on what performance is, as Glick, Washburn and Miller (2005) show.

In the same vein, Carneiro and Dib (2006) state that empirical results on the determinants of business performance have been conflicting, among other possible reasons, due to inappropriate approaches used to conceptualise and measure the phenomenon.

In the same vein, Neely, Gregory and Platts (2005) also state that performance measurement is a much-discussed but rarely defined topic. Literally, it is the process of quantifying action, where measurement is the process of quantification and action leads to performance.

Some management scholars have provided examples of divergent definitions of performance, such as: "profit maximisation, or more precisely, present value"; or "high returns over long periods of time"; or "rate of return on assets"; or "simple results based on financial indicators" (Johnston, Wade and McClean, 2007; Ferreira, Goldszmidt and Csillag, 2010; Mithas, Ramasubbu and Sambamurthy, 2011; Gomez and Pather, 2012;

Mustafa, 2015).

As Venkatraman and Ramanujam (1986) also point out, although performance is a recurring theme that interests both managers and scientists, defining what performance is is also one of the thorniest issues in academic research. The volume of literature on the subject is growing, which does not give us much hope of reaching an agreement or consensus on basic terminology and definitions.

The same authors also present a model of the scope covered by the firm's performance, in which the narrowest concept is that of financial performance, based on financial indicators (e.g. sales growth, profitability expressed by return on investment, return on sales), which reflect the fulfilment of the firm's financial targets.

However, as Chakravarthy (1986) shows us, there are some key measures for measuring performance, but it doesn't seem to be true that a single measure can correctly assess performance; hence the author's suggestion of adopting some multidimensional factor.

In the study published by the authors Bharadwaj, Bharadwaj and Konsynski (1999) on how IT contributes to company performance, once again we see financial indicators used to measure performance, in this case Tobin's Q was mentioned as a good measure, and the authors conclude that investments in IT contribute to better company financial performance.

With similar reasoning, Wernerfelt and Montgomery (1988), in their work on the importance of focus for business performance, also use Tobin's Q to measure performance.

Within this divergent way of looking at performance, scholars March and Sutton (1997) provide interesting perspectives and show that many organisational performance studies define performance as a dependent variable and seek to identify variables that produce variations in performance, which, according to the authors, does not take into account various complications, such as the instability of the competitive advantage that comes from better performance and the complexity of the environment as a whole.

The authors go on to say that these complications are well known to scholars on the subject, but that despite this, they continue to use this standard due to the very context of organisational research, which, on the one hand, demands and rewards speculation on how to improve organisational performance and, on the other, demands and rewards strict adherence to academic research standards.

Similarly, Brito (2007) states that business performance is still a construct in search of a more precise definition and consensus among researchers. For the author, one of the central issues is the dimensionality of this performance and, consequently, how to measure each of its dimensions. Based on a survey of Brazilian managers, the author comes to the conclusion that the financial performance dimension ends up being the most studied.

Based on empirical work analysing the results of 252 Brazilian companies between 1998 and 2001, Brito and Vasconcelos (2004) conclude that superior or inferior performance is not uncommon; they also warn us that company performance, contrary to what the neoclassical economic model predicts, is highly heterogeneous.

For the aforementioned authors Neely, Gregory and Platts (2005), performance can be measured in relation to various factors - quality, time, cost and flexibility - as Magutu, Muganda and Ondimu (2011) also show in a survey of commercial banks in Kenya.

For Coppeland, Koller and Murrin (2004), the increased importance of shareholders in most developed countries has led a growing number of managers to focus on value creation as the most important measure of corporate performance. In this respect, the evidence suggests that concentrating on company value is significant both for shareholders and for the economy and other stakeholders.

Ceolin (2006) argues that information is the basic input in the decision-making process for investing in assets and, in recent decades, the creation of value and the performance of companies has become a matter of interest at all levels of the market.

Melville, Kraemer and Gurbaxani (2004) also list the value of IT's impact on organisational performance, including improved productivity, ability to make a profit, cost reduction, competitive advantage, inventory reduction and other performance measures. The authors cite the following criteria as examples of metrics for measuring company performance associated with the use of IT: customer satisfaction, stock turnover, on-time delivery, cost reduction, increased revenue, competitive advantage and the company's market value.

The literature on the subject also addresses a question prior to analysing IT spending and investment, raising the issue of what purpose IT is used for, so that we can compare equivalent dimensions, leading us to the concept of converting IT into results (Weill, 2006; Albertin, 2009; Mithas et al., 2012).

In the context of small and medium-sized enterprises, the discussion of IT performance and effectiveness is also present in various studies, such as Chinomona's (2013), which, through a survey of 162 SMEs in Zimbabwe, shows the positive influence of IT on companies' strategic purchases, logistics integration and the consequent impact on company performance; or Loeser, Erek and Zarnekow (2012), who, based on the evaluation of a business performance measurement system with a multi-criteria decision analysis, conclude that the use of IT has led to the optimisation of processes and an increase in organisational efficiency, which has generated a greater degree of competitiveness.

In the same vein, Riascos and Aguilera (2011), in a study of 60 companies in the industrial, commercial and service sectors in Santiago de Cali (Colombia), showed that the use of IT improved company productivity, generating better performance. Mithas, Ramasubbu and Sambamurthy (2011), in a study of 80 industrial companies, found a positive influence of IT use on business performance in three specific perspectives: customer management, process management and financial results.

Similarly, in an empirical study of 74 Colombian SMEs, Pérez, Garzón and Nieto (2009) show that the use of IT positively affects the financial indicators of companies, but at the same time has no impact on their productivity; in a study of 400 SMEs in Aguas Calientes (Mexico), Maldonado et al. (2010) show that the use of IT has a positive influence on company profits; and Nakata, Zhu and Kraimer (2008) conclude in their study of 189 companies from different regions of the United States that the use of IT indirectly influences company profits by strengthening customer management.

Although the subject has been widely studied, we cannot say that there is a clear and direct understanding of the relationship between IT spending and investment and performance. For this reason, the literature on the subject contains papers that define IT and business value in very different ways, with various ways of assessing the impact of IT on performance (Callahan, Gabriel and Smith, 2009; Seddon, Calvert and Yang, 2010; Flyvbjerg and Budzier, 2011; Albarracín, Erazo and Palacios, 2014).

As we can see from the references above, there are many studies relating performance to IT effectiveness and resulting in tangible improvements (cost reduction, increased revenue and profitability) and intangible improvements (improved productivity and greater capacity for innovation).

It was in Weill's work (1992) that the concept of effective IT conversion or conversion effectiveness emerged, highlighting the need to separate the different types of investment and combine them with appropriate organisational performance measures. Later, Weill and Broadbent (1998) further categorised IT needs (objectives) into informational, strategic, transactional and infrastructure needs. And the subject continues to evolve with several other studies with some variations (Lucas, 1999; McKeen, Smith and Parent, 1999; Dehning and Richardson, 2002), but all the research models presented in these studies come close in terms of disclosure, recognising that IT investments have an effect or impact on company performance.

In this study, the financial performance dimension was adopted as the performance measure, as Lefebvre; Mason and Lefebvre (1997) did, because it is a widely accepted measure that is easy to measure, since we consider both information on companies' revenue and net profit, as well as intangible aspects, measured by managers' perceptions of the impact of IT use on cost reduction, productivity and innovation capacity.

3.3 Small and medium-sized enterprises (SMEs)

Small and medium-sized companies play an important role in economic and social development around the world, and many studies have pointed out how one cannot want to analyse this type of company through the same lens used to analyse large corporations (Parker and Castleman, 2007; Arendt, 2008; Devos, Landeghem and Deschoolmeester, 2012; Bayo-Moriones, Billón and Lera-López, 2013). In the case of Brazilian companies, the work of Prates and Ospina (2004) also contributes in the same direction.

A first fundamental issue for small and medium-sized enterprises concerns the time and resources available when they start up, which in most cases are scarce, leading to the need for good performance to be of crucial importance for their survival, as demonstrated in the work of Chinomona (2013).

When we talk about the use of IT by SMEs, as Lucchetti and Sterlacchini (2004) did, we are referring to the general use of IT (internet, integrated management systems), technologies that integrate production in some way (supply chain management tools), as well as market-orientated technologies (customer management tools).

When we look at SMEs in developing countries, as is the case in Brazil, the importance of good IT use increases, especially if the company is to be truly inserted into the knowledge economy, whether by developing supply channels or sales channels, as Piget and Kossai (2013) point out in their work with SMEs in Tunisia.

However, a major difficulty encountered by SMEs is the issue of access to technology, which is more strongly felt in developing countries, where presence in locations with more companies tends to improve this deficiency (Steinfield et al., 2012).

Also highlighting the barriers to access and adoption of IT by SMEs, Arendt's work (2008) divides the main difficulties into four:

1) lack of basic experience caused by disinterest, as well as a lack of attraction to new technologies,

called "mental access";

2) physical absence of computers and connections, the so-called "material access";

3) lack of digital skills caused by inadequate education and social support, the so-called "skills gap";

4) absence of significant opportunities for use, called "access to use".

However, on the other hand, if it doesn't solve all these issues regarding the barriers to access and adoption of IT by SMEs, at least to alleviate them we can see today the abundant presence of new business models which, as *is* the case with so-called "cloud computing", with more affordable conditions, enable greater access to technology for SMEs too, especially in developing countries, as also shown by the work of Albarracín, Erazo and Palacios (2014) carried out with 1,201 Colombian SMEs.

Baines (1999) presents an interesting paper in which he analyses the role of technology in very small companies, often made up of just one person, even using teleworking and operating in virtual organisations, such as those already mentioned by Albertin (2010) and Stanworth (1998), which can only gain access to new technologies through these new business models.

When we think about the impact that the use of IT can have on the performance of SMEs, some of the determining factors are the perceived importance and commitment to adoption of top management, more specifically the owner of the company, as well as public policies (Consoli, 2012).

In Brazil, according to Decree 6.022 of 22/01/2007, the Public Digital Bookkeeping System (SPED) was made available to companies, making it compulsory for companies to present tax information in digital form, as a result of which small Brazilian companies also had to somehow seek greater computerisation.

Still in the context of small and medium-sized companies, Lefebvre, Mason and Lefebvre (1997) demonstrate the power of the CEO's perception of the company's environment in defining technology policy and how this has a moderating effect on the company's results.

The work by Southern and Tilley (2000) also follows the path of pointing out the main determinants of technology adoption in small and medium-sized companies, and once again we see the importance of the owner's or chief executive's perception of the role that technology plays in the company as an important factor.

There are various definitions of what small, medium and micro enterprises are, varying in terms of the number of employees and turnover (European Commission, 2003; Devos, Landeghem and Deschoolmeester, 2008). SEBRAE - the Brazilian Micro and Small Business Support Service - also classifies micro and small businesses according to the length of time the company has been in existence, calling it TEA - Early Stage Entrepreneurship Rate (SEBRAE, 2014) and showing an interesting relationship between the length of time the company has been in existence and the use of current technologies.

3.4 Perceptions of the stages of computerisation and the role of IT

With regard to the literature review, we can find various approaches to the role of IT in organisations, such as diagnostic models, which provide instruments and criteria for diagnosing the role of IT in organisations. In this category, we can mention a few: The Analysis of IT Centralisation and Decentralisation (Buchanan and Linowes, 1980 and Donovan, 1988); Information Intensity Matrix (Porter and Millar, 1985); Relationship between IT Investments and Organisational Performance (Mahmood, 1993; Byrd and Marshall, 1997); The Strategic Alignment Model (Henderson and Venkatraman, 1993; Luftman, Lewis and Oldach, 1993). This group includes work by Nolan (1979) on the Stages of Computerisation of Companies, in which he proposes six stages (initiation, contagion, control, integration, management and maturity) shown in **Figure 1**.

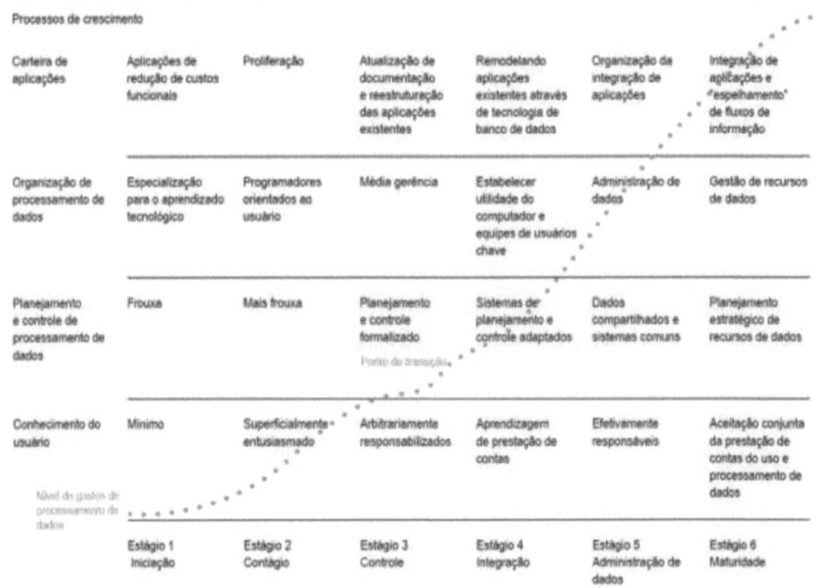

Figura 1 - Six stages of data processing growth Source: Adapted from Nolan (1979).

In addition, the model initially proposed by McFarlan (1984), shown in Figure 2, makes it possible to visualise how IT is related to the company's business strategy and operations. This model analyses the impact of current and future IT applications on the business, defining four "quadrants" that represent *the* situation for *the* company, with the following definitions:

Support - IT has little influence on the company's current and future strategies. There is no need for the IT department to have a prominent position in the company hierarchy. This is usually what happens in traditional manufacturing.

Factory - Existing IT applications make a decisive contribution to the company's success, but there are no plans for new applications with a strategic impact. The IT department must be positioned at a high hierarchical level. The classic example is airlines, which depend on their ticket booking systems, but new developments only update these applications.

Transition - IT moves from a more discreet situation ("support" quadrant) to one of greater prominence in the company's strategy. The IT area tends towards a position of greater importance in the company's hierarchy. The example usually cited in the literature is desktop publishing. Today, *e-commerce* has the same profile, moving from a support role in the operation of a commercial company to being a transforming agent in the business.

Strategic - IT has a major influence on the company's overall strategy. Both current and future applications are strategic, affecting the company's business. In this case, it is important that IT is positioned at a high level in the hierarchical structure. In banks, for example, IT plays this strategic role.

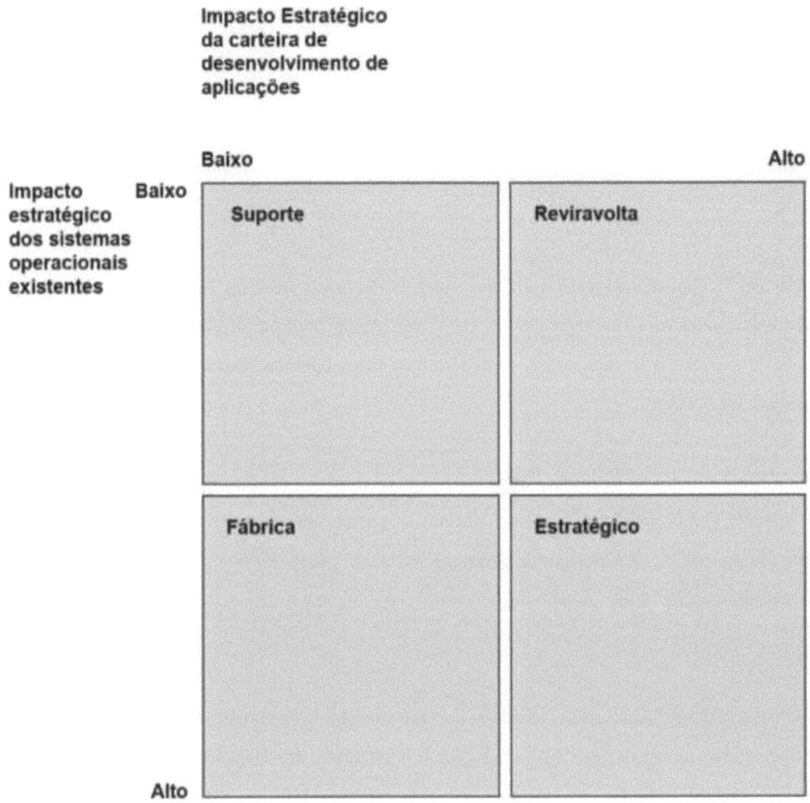

Figure 2 - Position of Information Systems

Source: Adapted from McFarlan (1984).

These two authors developed another interesting model, called the "IT Strategic Impact Grid" (Nolan and McFarlan, 2005), shown in **Figure 3**, in which they present developments in their theories with interesting indications for better governance of IT activities.

Figure 3 - IT strategic impact grid

Source: Adapted from Nolan and McFarlan (2005).

Another interesting methodology, which we have also taken into account in this work, is that developed by the research and consulting company Gartner, the so-called "Magic Quadrant", as presented in the work by Stang and Duggan (2015), which offers a snapshot, in-depth analyses and practical recommendations that provide information on the direction, maturity and players in a market. Magic Quadrants compare suppliers based on a two-dimensional matrix that assesses their breadth of vision and ability to execute, as exemplified in **Figure 4**.

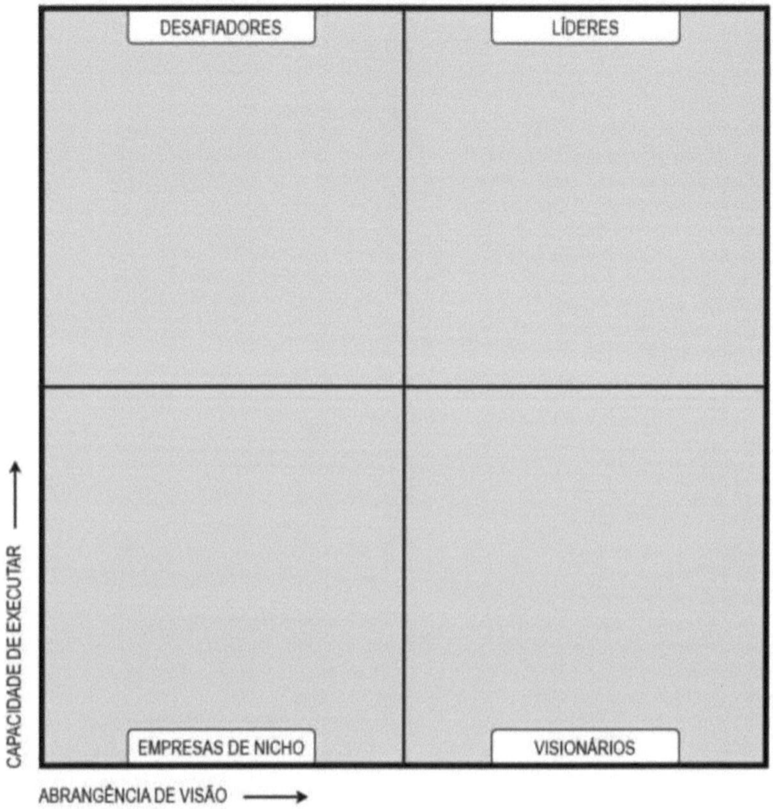

Figure 4 - Gartner Magic Quadrant

Source: Adapted from Gartner (2015)

This model developed by Gartner presents four groups of suppliers:

- "Leaders": greater breadth of vision and high capacity for execution;

- "Challengers": high execution capacity and smaller scope of vision;

- "Visionaries": greater breadth of vision and low capacity for execution;

- "Niche companies": low execution capacity and smaller scope of vision.

Another very relevant reference for the development of this research was obtained in the work of Lefebvre, Mason and Lefebvre (1997), in which the authors propose a model that takes into account the perception of the manager and the performance of the company, focussing precisely on small and medium-sized companies with a maximum of 200 employees. They used a sample of 84 companies from the industrial sector in the Quebec region (Canada).

In this research we have developed concepts based on these studies, applied to the context of small and medium-sized Brazilian companies. We chose this because we believe that the combination of these concepts, combined with the verification of the level of IT spending, can point to interesting patterns, with indications of best practices for obtaining better results from the use of IT.

CHAPTER 4

Methodology

The methodology adopted involves the application of questionnaires to obtain both quantitative data on the profile of IT use and financial information and qualitative data on the perception of the role IT plays in companies.

This part of the work presents the methodological approach and the steps taken to carry out the empirical research and fulfil the objectives of the thesis.

4.1 Methodological approach

In this thesis, the approach adopted is positivist, as it assumes that reality is objective, whose premise is the existence of a phenomenon (the use of IT by companies) related to an outcome (company performance), which will be investigated with a predefined instrument (questionnaire), in order to draw inferences about a phenomenon based on the sample for the stated population (Orlikowski and Baroudi, 1991). This perspective has been the dominant one in the field of Information Systems studies.

As discussed by Piccoli and Ives (2005), the research focus consists of a specific IT initiative as the unit of analysis. In the case of this study, the obligation imposed by the Brazilian government for companies to submit their tax information digitally can help minimise the effect of other variables on the result.

The aim of this thesis is to explore the context of IT use and company performance, using as variables the perception of the role IT plays in the company, the level of maturity in IT use and the volume of IT spending.

A recurring issue when it comes to linking IT spending and investment to company performance is the difficulty of isolating other factors that may also have an impact on the result, so that it becomes difficult to show the impact of IT use alone.

In order to address this issue, researchers in the field have made progress in relating IT value in particular to capabilities for improving company performance (Devaraj and Kohli, 2003; Aral and Weill, 2007; Kohli and Grover, 2008; Mithas et al., 2012).

In the same vein, we focus on the impact that IT can have on some specific capabilities, leading to benefits such as cost reduction, increased productivity and innovation and the creation of new products and services, according to the model proposed by Albertin and Albertin (2012) shown in **Figure 5**.

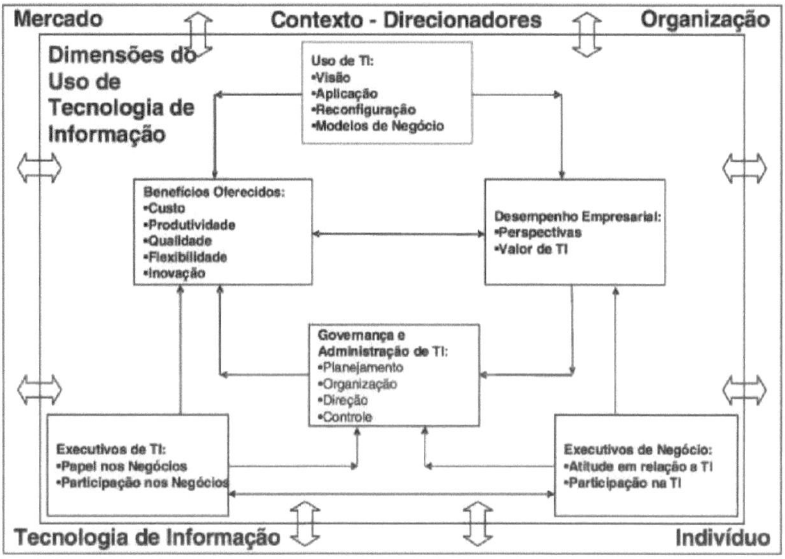

Figure 5 - Dimensions of the use of Information Technology to benefit business Source: Albertin and Albertin (2012).

This quantitative study, of an applied nature and descriptive-explanatory objective (Collis and Hussey, 2005; Creswel, 2009; Hair et al., 2011), used a survey-type procedure (Groves et al. 2004), applying the cluster analysis technique, operationalised in accordance with the indications of Hair et al. (2010). Cluster analysis aims to group objects with similar characteristics, making it possible to assess the behaviour of the groups according to the discriminating variables.

4.2 Research model

According to the literature review, a model was drawn up that would best serve the purpose of the research, which aims to verify whether there is an association between IT spending and investment and the performance of small and medium-sized companies, mediated by managers' perceptions of the role that IT plays in the company, as shown in **Figure 6**. In addition, to verify the possibility of separating companies into groups and examining these resulting groups to see if there are distinct types and, if so, what their characteristics are (Aaker, Kumar and Day, 2010).

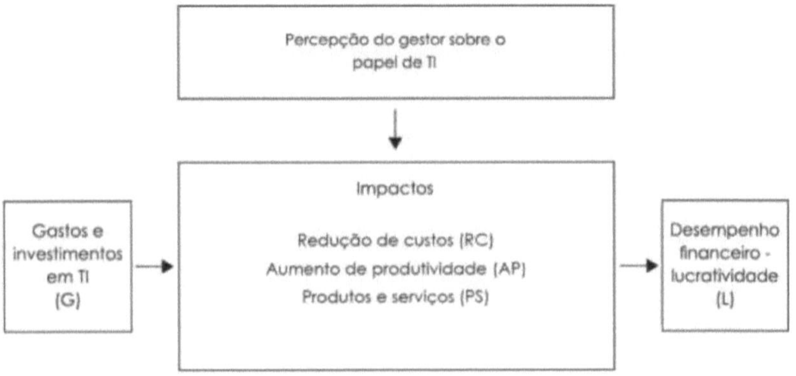

Figure 6 - Conceptual model of the study

Source: Prepared by the author

The proposed model was based on the aforementioned theories of maturity in the use of IT, the roles that IT plays in the business, the dimensions and benefits of using IT, and also on research into the use of IT (Nolan, 1979; McFarlan, 1984; Nolan and McFarlan, 2005; Albertin and Albertin, 2012; Meirelles, 2015), with the constructs shown in **Table 1**.

Table 1 - Constructs

MG	0 MG index is the average over three years (2012, 2013 and 2014) of total annual IT spending as a percentage of the company's net annual turnover. 0 Total spending is *the* sum of all investments, expenses and funds allocated to IT, including: equipment, facilities, supplies and consumables, software, services, teleprocessing and direct and indirect costs of own and third-party staff working on IT systems, support and training.
ML	0 ML index is the three-year average (2012, 2013 and 2014) of the company's annual net profit in relation to its net turnover.
HRC	Managers' perception of the impact of IT today on cost reduction.
HAP	Managers' perception of the impact of IT today on increasing productivity.
HPS	Managers' perception of the impact of IT on products and services today.
FRC	Managers' perception of the impact of IT in the future on cost reduction.
FAP	Managers' perception of the impact of IT in the future on increasing productivity.
FPS	Managers' perception of the future impact of IT on products and services.

IE	Managers' perception of the strategic impact of IT on business in the future.
IF	Managers' perception of the impact of legal changes on IT spending and investment.

Source: Prepared by the author

In this model we relate the constructs referring to managers' perception of benefits such as cost reduction, increased productivity, products and services, the role that IT plays in the company, whether it can be considered strategic or not, with financial data on IT spending and investment and with profitability.

4.3 Sample

The population of this survey was made up of organisations from a variety of sectors, whose respondents are professionals in management positions, who were participants in postgraduate business courses throughout Brazil, with a total of 420 responses from companies located in 130 different municipalities and in 14 states of the federation, as shown in **Table 2**, making it a fairly representative sample of the conditions in companies in Brazil as a whole (Kohli, Devaraj and Ow, 2012; Ouakouak and Ouedraogo, 2013).As a first step, descriptive statistics were used to process the data collected, checking the mean, maximum, minimum, standard deviation and mode. This made it possible to check for discrepancies arising, for example, from collection errors, which resulted in 14 questionnaires with incomplete answers being disregarded, considered missing values and excluded from the sample, which led us to a final figure of 406 valid answers.

Table 2 - Municipalities where the companies surveyed are located

City	State	City	State
Acreúna	GO	Monte Mor	SP
Adolfo	SP	Nepomuceno	MG
Águas de São Pedro	SP	New Venice	SC
Anísio de Abreu	PI	Olympia	SP
Aparecida do Norte	SP	Orlândia	SP
Araraquara	SP	Orleans	SC
Atibaia	SP	Osasco	SP
Barueri	SP	Paraguaçu Paulista	SP
Drinking fountain	SP	Paulínia	SP
Bento Gonçalves	RS	Pereira Barreto	SP
Birigui	SP	Piracaia	SP
Bom Jesus das Selvas	MA	Pirapozinho	SP
Cachoeira de Minas	MG	Fallen Wells	MG
Campaign	MG	Porecatu	PR
Campinas	SP	Porto Alegre	RS
Capivari de Baixo	SC	Porto Ferreira	SP
Carlos Barbosa	RS	Pradópolis	SP
Carolina	MA	President Bernardes	SP
Rattlesnake	EC	President Prudente	SP
Catanduva	SP	Quatá	SP
Caxias do Sul	RS	Quirinópolis	GO
Cocai do Sul	SC	Ribeirão Preto	SP
Counting	MG	Rio de Janeiro	RJ
Cotia	SP	Green River	GO

Cravinhos	SP	Jump	SP
Criciúma	SC	Salvador	BA
Curitiba	PR	Santa Barbara do Oeste	SP
Diadema	SP	Santa Branca	SP
Embú das Artes	SP	Santa Cruz do Sul	RS
Espírito Santo do Pinhal	SP	Santa Maria	RS
Farroupilha	RS	Santa Rosa do Viterbo	SP
Flores da Cunha	RS	Santana de Parnaíba	SP
Florianópolis	SC	Saint Anastasius	SP
Forklift	SC	St Andrew's	SP
France	SP	Santo Antonio da Patrulha	RS
Goiânia	GO	Santos	SP
Guarulhos	SP	São Bernardo do Campo	SP
Guaxupé	MG	São Caetano do Sul	SP
Ibiraiaras	RS	São Carlos	SP
Ibitinga	SP	São Joaquim da Barra	SP
Içara	SC	São José do Rio Preto	SP
Empress	MA	São José Dos Campos	SP
Itajubá	MG	São Leopoldo	RS
Itanhandú	MG	St Mark's	RS
Itapecerica da Serra	SP	São Paulo	SP
Itu	SP	São Sebastião	SP
Jaboticabal	SP	Sertãozinho	SP
Jacareí	SP	Siderópolis	SC
Jataí	GO	Dark	SC
Joinville	SC	Sorocaba	SP
Jundiaí	SP	Taboão da Serra	SP
Lajeado	RS	Taciba	SP
Laranjal Paulista	SP	Teodoro Sampaio	SP
Lins	SP	Toledo	PR
Maceio	AL	Tres Lagoas	MS
Manaus	AM	Shark	SC
Marília	SP	Tupandi	RS
Matão	SP	Turvo	SC
Mauá	SP	Uberaba	MG
Mococa	SP	Uberlândia	MG
Mogi das Cruzes	SP	Urussanga	SC
Monte Alto	SP	Vacaria	RS
Monte Aprazível	SP	Vargem Grande Paulista	SP
Monte Azul Paulista	SP	Vespasian	MG
Monte Belo	MG	Votuporanga	SP

Source: Prepared by the author

Since we are only interested in companies considered small and medium-sized, which, for the purposes of this study, are those with a maximum of 700 keyboards in use, as considered in Meirelles (2015). We got a total of 361 valid responses, of which 322 were from small companies (those with up to 170 keyboards), of which 244 had less than 30 keyboards; and 39 medium-sized companies, those with between 171 and 700 keyboards in use, as shown in **Graph 1.**

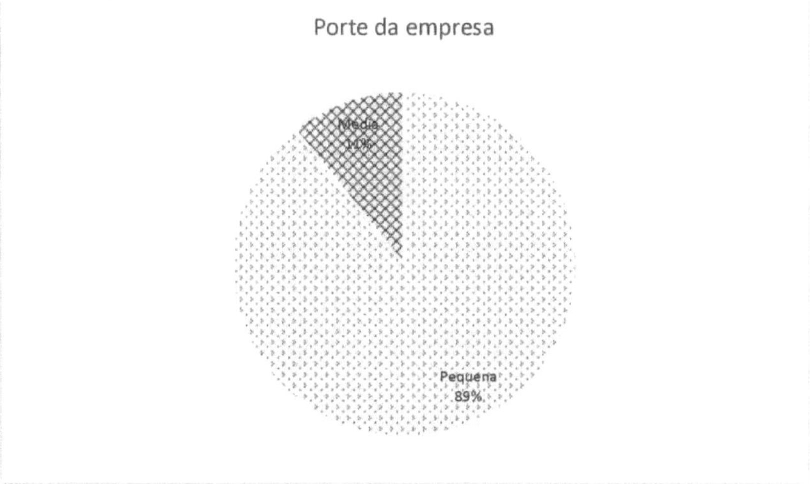

Graph 1 - Company size

Source: Prepared by the author

The research identified the perceptions of managers (Sekaran, 2000) on aspects related to the use of IT and the resulting benefits, capturing multiple perspectives of business performance. Thus, the sample was heterogeneous (Lunardi, Becker and Maçada, 2012) across different types of organisations and with managers from different areas and hierarchical positions. Despite being a non-probabilistic convenience sample, which leaves it up to the researcher to select the sample units according to their convenience, through which operational viability is achieved (Aaker, Kumar and Day, 2010), the sample proved to be of very high quality, given that the respondents had at least five years' experience in management and knowledge of the research constructs.

4.4 Data collection

The instrument defined for data collection was the questionnaire, which was answered after being explained in class about the proposed questions, clarifying doubts and thus bringing quality to the answers.

Initially, a pilot questionnaire (**Appendix A**) was drawn up based on the literature review, in order to comply with the guidelines on content validity, the number of categories, the number of items to measure the constructs, the choice of scale, the compulsory nature of the answers and the type of label used in the categories, as recommended by Hair et al. (2010).

To validate the instrument, experts (researchers, professors, industry executives) with many years of experience in the IT field gave their opinions and contributed to improving the quality of the questionnaire.

The following suggestions were accepted:

-reduction of the research period from five to three years, in order to facilitate the collection of data;

-decreasing the number of questions to capture the respondents' perception of the strategic role of IT, from sixteen to eight questions;

-changes in the wording of some questions to make them easier to understand;

-changing the scale from five points to four points to simplify data collection and processing.

After validation by the experts, we arrived at the final questionnaire used in this study (**Appendix B**). A pre-test was then carried out and the questionnaire was applied to a sample of 52 managers, which meets the minimum sample size recommendations for pre-tests, which ranges from 15 to 25 respondents (Aaker, Kumar and Day, 2010).

A web-based questionnaire solution called Survey Monkey (https://www.surveymonkey.com/) was also used to operationalise the collection. This allows a survey instrument to be constructed and made available via web links, thus facilitating data collection, which took place between May and October 2015.

The questionnaires were made up of two distinct parts: the first to collect (confidential) company registration data, as well as figures relating to their financial performance over the last three years (2012 to 2014), in a similar way to that in Meirelles (2015); and the second, made up of eight questions, to find out company managers' perceptions of the role IT plays in the business, whose development process followed the work of Moore and Benbasat (1991).

The first part of the questionnaire includes both registration information (company name, CNPJ, address, sector and branch of activity, name, position and e-mail address of the respondent) and information about the size and results of the company over the last three years (from 2012 to 2014) - total number of employees, net annual revenue, net annual profit, total IT spending, total number of company devices (keyboards in use) - and about the year in which the company started using IT.

The second part of the questionnaire contains six questions to gauge the respondents' perceptions of the role and contribution of IT in the company, specifically with regard to reducing costs, increasing productivity and the impact of IT on new products and services, both now and in the future. The answers were measured using a 4-point *Likert* scale, ranging from "strongly disagree" to "strongly agree", as several other studies have done (Barros and Nahas, 2001, Rajanen, Salminen and Ravaja, 2015; Wu et al., 2015).

And to finalise the instrument, they were also asked about their perception of the impact of IT on the company's performance in general in the future and also about the impact that legal obligations to use IT have had on companies. Likewise, the answers were measured using a 4-point *Likert* scale, ranging from "totally disagree" to "totally agree".

4.5 Statistical treatment of data

Given the aim of this study, to see if there is an association between IT spending and investment and the performance of small and medium-sized enterprises, mediated by managers' perceptions of the stages of computerisation and the role that IT plays in the company, it is appropriate to classify the sample collected into homogeneous groups according to perceptions and patterns of spending and results; this is how the so-called cluster analysis technique was chosen.

According to this technique, the similarity between individuals from the same group must be greater than that between individuals from different groups, i.e. individuals from different groups must differ significantly from each other.

Cluster analysis is an exploratory technique in which no prior definition is made regarding the number of groups or their structure. The groupings are based on similarities or distances (dissimilarities). Classifying companies into homogeneous groups identifies the differences in profile between them, which also makes it possible to explore more effectively the behaviour of the variables considered in the group of individuals and the relationships between these individuals. As well as conveniently summarising the information contained, this exploratory work makes it possible to develop or confirm hypotheses relating to these individuals or variables (Corrar, Paulo and Dias Filho, 2009).

In order to classify into different groups, it is necessary to define which variables will be used, since the classification will depend on the variables chosen.

The variables used to separate the clusters are called drivers, and the variables used to describe each cluster are the discriminator variables.

In the case of this study, the driving variables are as follows: average IT spending (MG); average relative profit (ML); managers' perception of the impact of IT today on cost reduction (HRC); managers' perception of the impact of IT today

on increased productivity (HAP); managers' perception of the impact of IT today on products and services (HPS); managers' perception of the impact of IT in the future on cost reduction (FRC); managers' perception of the impact of IT in the future on increased productivity (FAP); managers' perception of the impact of IT in the future on products and services (FPS).

And the discriminating variables are: the company's sector of operation; average number of employees; average annual net revenue; length of time the company has been using IT; managers' perception of the strategic impact of IT in the future (IE); and managers' perception of the impact of legal changes on IT spending and investment (IF).

For all eight variables relating to the perception of managers, a 4-point Likert scale was used (4= Strongly agree; 3= Partially agree; 2= Partially disagree; 1= Strongly disagree), which, for the purposes of statistical treatment, were considered quantitative, ranging from 1 to 4.

With regard to the selection of guiding variables relating to the perception of the role that IT plays in the company, we started with a total of six variables that we included in the questionnaire. After an initial analysis of the data, especially with regard to the correlation between these variables, as illustrated in **Table 3**, it seemed interesting to see if it would be possible to reduce the number of variables to a smaller number that would be sufficient to represent the impact of IT, since the aim is to measure the specific impact in three dimensions: cost reduction, increased productivity and new products and services, both in the present and in the future, as presented in the theory on the subject that served as the basis for creating the questionnaire.

Table 3 - Correlation between perception variables

Correlation: HRC; HAP; HPS; FRC; FAP; FPS

	HRC	HAP	HPS	FRC	FAP
HAP	0, 628				
	0,000				
HPS	0,560	0,567			
	0,000	0,000			
FRC	0,790	0, 611	0,522		
	0,000	0,000	0,000		
FAP	0, 608	0,825	0,501	0,727	
	0,000	0,000	0,000	0,000	
FPS	0,529	0,538	0,833	0,593	0,599
	0,000	0,000	0,000	0,000	0,000

Cell Contents: Pearson correlation
P-Value

Source: Prepared by the author using Minitab 17 statistical software.

To carry out this procedure of reducing the number of variables, the factor analysis technique was applied, which is based on the assumption that the correlation between variables arises because these variables share or are related by the same factor (Corrar, Paulo and Dias Filho, 2009; Aaker, Kumar and Day, 2010; Hair et al., 2010), initially analysing the correlation matrix between the six variables, which showed a high degree of correlation between some variables, as can be seen in **Table 3**, indicating the possibility of reduction.

Moving on to the application of the factor analysis technique, the method chosen was the most common, called Principal Component Analysis, which looks for a linear combination between the variables so that the maximum amount of variance is explained by this combination. And, as Hair et al. (2010) emphasise, this should be the method chosen when the aim is for a minimum number of factors to explain the maximum amount of variance in the original variables and when prior knowledge of the variables suggests that the specific variance and error represent a small part of the explanation of the total variance of the variables.

Using Minitab 17 statistical software, and at first considering all six variables, we arrived at the result shown in **Table 4**, in which three factors are sufficient to explain more than 90 per cent of the variance with regard to the perception of the role IT plays in the company. Furthermore, according to another rule of thumb related to this subject, exactly between factors 3 and 4, there is a large drop in the variance explained between both factors; in this case, the choice of the number of factors should be cut at this point.

Table 4 - Factor analysis with six variables

Factor Analysis: HRC; HAP; HPS; FRC; FAP; FPS

Principal Component Factor Analysis of the Correlation Matrix

Unrotated Factor Loadings and Communalities

Variable	Factor1	Factor2	Factor3	Factor4	Factor5	Factor6	Communality
HRC	0,826	0,213	0,419	-0,257	-0,170	0,040	1,000
HAP	0,838	0,237	-0,390	-0,248	0,054	-0,159	1,000
HPS	0, 793	-0,545	-0,001	-0,175	0,167	0,130	1,000
FRC	0,854	0,247	0,317	0,251	0,201	-0,072	1,000
FAP	0,859	0,288	-0,312	0,202	-0,076	0,190	1,000
FPS	0,817	-0,492	-0,027	0,207	-0,175	-0,128	1,000
Variance	4,1461	0,7846	0,5263	0,3049	0,1366	0,1015	6,0000
% Chg	0,691	0,131	0,088	0,051	0,023	0,017	1,000

Source: Prepared by the author using Minitab 17 statistical software.

In order to explain the meaning of each factor, it is necessary to analyse the factor analysis parameters that relate the factors to the variables, the so-called **factor loadings**. For the best results in terms of interpretation, it is recommended to rotate the factors, as there are various rotation methods that allow you to obtain factors with greater potential for interpretation, and the most widely used is the **Varimax** method, which we used in this work and whose results can be seen in **Table 5** (Corrar, Paulo and Dias Filho, 2009).

As we can see, Factor 1 represents the variables HPS (managers' perception of the impact of IT on products and services today) and FPS (managers' perception of the impact of IT on products and services in the future); Factor 2 represents the variables HAP (managers' perception of the impact of IT today on increased productivity) and FAP (managers' perception of the impact of IT in the future on increased productivity); and Factor 3 represents the variables HRC (managers' perception of the impact of IT today on cost reduction) and FRC (managers' perception of the impact of IT in the future on cost reduction).

Table 5 - Factor analysis with three variables and Varimax rotation

Factor Analysis: HRC; HAP; HPS; FRC; FAP; FPS				
Principal Component Factor Analysis of the Correlation Matrix				
Unrotated Factor Loadings and Communalities				
Variable	Factor1	Factor2	Factor3	Communality
HRC	0,826	0,213	0,419	0,904
HAP	0,838	0,237	-0,390	0,911
HPS	0, 793	-0,545	-0,001	0,925
FRC	0,854	0,247	0,317	0,891
FAP	0,859	0,288	-0,312	0,917
FPS	0,817	-0,492	-0,027	0,910
Variance	4,1461	0,7846	0,5263	5,4570
% Chg	0, 691	0,131	0,088	0,910
Rotated Factor Loadings and Communalities Varimax Rotation				
Variable	Factor1	Factor2	Factor3	Communality
HRC	0,283	-0,286	-0,861	0,904
HAP	0,293	-0,860	-0,291	0,911
HPS	0,899	-0,232	-0,252	0,925
FRC	0,274	-0,388	-0,816	0,891
FAP	0,260	-0,841	-0,378	0,917
FPS	0,870	-0,286	-0,267	0,910
Variance	1,8729	1,8147	1,7694	5,4570
% Chg	0,312	0,302	0,295	0,910

Source: Prepared by the author using Minitab 17 statistical software.

As is well explained in the theory on the subject (Corrar, Paulo and Dias Filho, 2009; Aaker, Kumar and Day, 2010; Hair et al., 2010), before starting the process of classification into clusters, it is necessary to: 1) exclude the so-called outliers; 2) define how the similarity between the objects will be measured; and 3) decide whether the data should be standardised.

With regard to item 1 mentioned above, cluster analysis is very sensitive to the inclusion of irrelevant variables, as well as outliers or suspect data (objects that are very different from the others). Outliers can represent observations, called true "anomalies", which are not representative of the general population, and thus distort the true structure of the population.

Once again using Minitab 17 statistical software, as we can see in **Graph 2**, we didn't find any discrepant observations with regard to the ML variable - average relative profit; however, we did find six discrepant observations with regard to the MG variable - average IT spending, as shown in **Graph 3**.

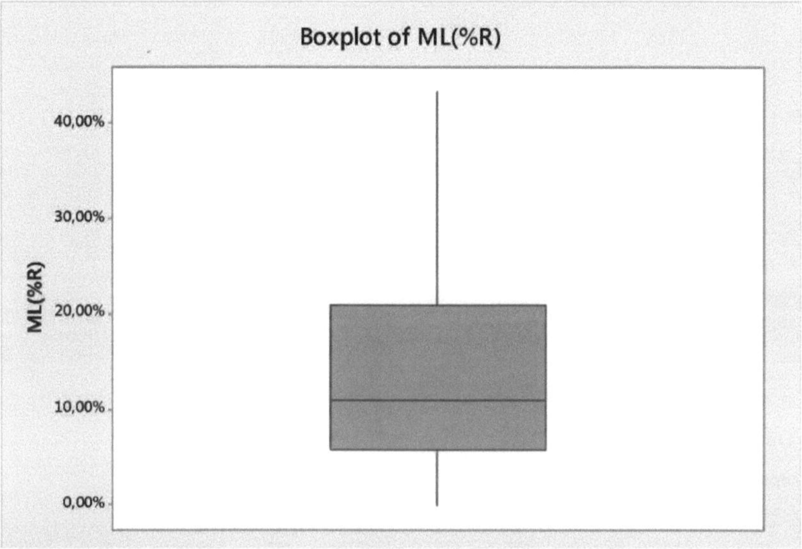

Graph 2 - Outlier analysis - ML variable

Source: Prepared by the author using Minitab 17 statistical software.

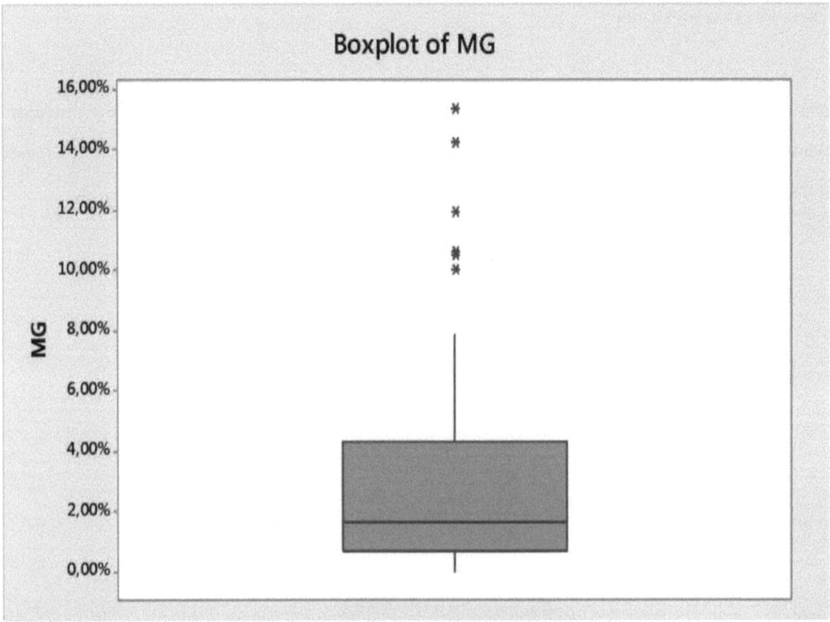

Graph 3 - Outlier analysis - variable MG

Source: Prepared by the author using Minitab 17 statistical software.

The six observations well above the average found for the MG variable - average IT spending - relate to six companies in the Information Technology area, which perhaps, by the very nature of their scope and market, have higher IT spending and investment; however, respecting the theory and aiming not to distort the structure, these six companies were removed from the sample, leaving this study with a total of 355 companies in its sample.

With regard to the second aspect mentioned in the theory and above, in order to group objects, some kind of measure of similarity or dissimilarity is needed, whereby similar objects are grouped together and the others are placed in separate conglomerates.

Similarity between objects can be measured in various ways, but three methods dominate cluster analysis applications: correlation measures, distance measures and association measures. Each of these methods represents a particular perspective on similarity, depending on the objects and the type of data. Correlation and distance measures require quantitative data, while association measures are for qualitative data.

In this research, in which the individuals (companies) are characterised by quantitative variables, we adopted the method of distance measures.

Distance measures are actually dissimilarity measures, with high values denoting lower similarity. Distance is converted into a measure of similarity by using an inverse relationship.

Various distance measures are available and the choice of distance measure depends on the type of scale of the variable. The most widely used is the Euclidean distance, which is also the one adopted in this work.

With regard to data standardisation, which is the next step in preparing to proceed with cluster analysis, we must understand that most distance measures, including the Euclidean, are totally sensitive to different scales or magnitude of variables, so it may be interesting to standardise the data, which we have adopted in this thesis based on the direct marking of such an option in the Minitab 17 statistical software when running the cluster analysis.

Once these preparatory requirements have been met, the next step should be to choose the cluster analysis method, which is nothing more than rules for grouping individuals that, in general, seek to fulfil two criteria:

- Great homogeneity within each cluster, i.e. the similarity between individuals in the same group should be as great as possible.

- Heterogeneity between clusters, i.e. the distance between each two groups should be as great as possible. In other words, we are looking for clusters that are very different from each other.

The methods should lead to "internal cohesion" and "isolation", as shown in Figure 7.

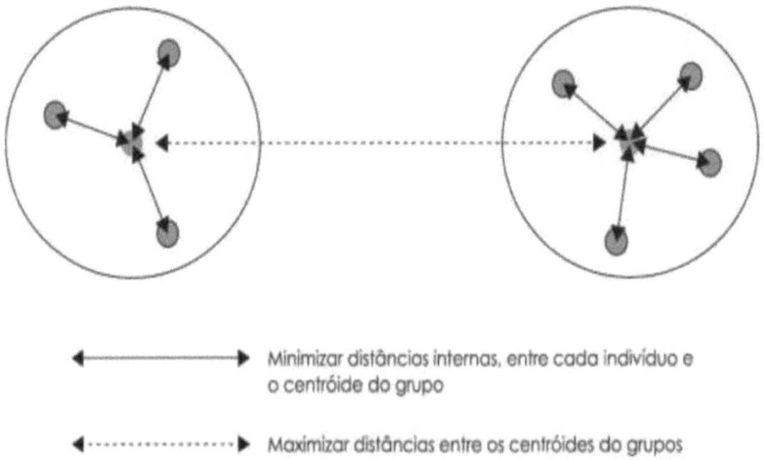

Figura 7 - Distances when grouping individuals
Source: Sicsú (1996)

There are many methods described in the literature on the subject (Corrar, Paulo and Dias Filho, 2009; Aaker, Kumar and Day, 2010; Hair et al., 2010), and the most widely used can be classified into two general categories: hierarchical and non-hierarchical. Hierarchical methods include agglomerative and divisive methods.

In hierarchical agglomerative methods, the "n" individuals initially define "n" groups; next, the two closest groups are merged and, so on, the groups are merged step by step until a single cluster is reached made up of all the "n" individuals. **Figure 8** illustrates the procedure for grouping individuals A, B, C, D and E.

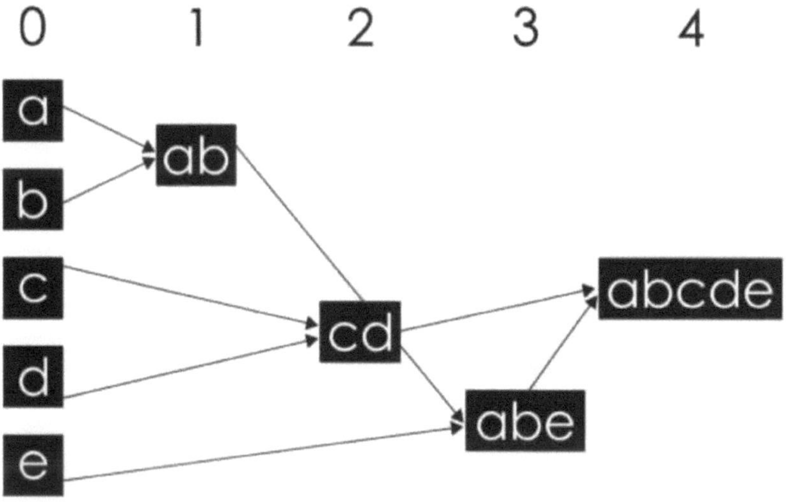

Figura 8 - Hierarchical agglomerative methods
Source: Sicsú (1996)

In hierarchical divisive methods, the "n" individuals initially define a single group; then this group is divided into two groups; then each of these is divided into another two groups and so on, until "n" groups are reached, each of which is made up of a single individual.

In non-hierarchical methods, arbitrary initial groups are formed and individuals are reallocated between groups until the configuration obtained optimises a previously defined criterion of internal homogeneity and/or heterogeneity between groups.

According to the literature consulted on the subject, it is not possible to definitively define which of the methods is the best, depending very much on the type of research and the context studied. The most popular are hierarchical techniques, as they are faster and require less processing time, and are also easier to read and interpret (Bussab, Miazaki and Andrade, 1990; Sharma, 1996; Sicsú, 1996; Corrar, Paulo and Dias Filho, 2009; Aaker, Kumar and Day, 2010). The hierarchical agglomerative method was also adopted in this study.

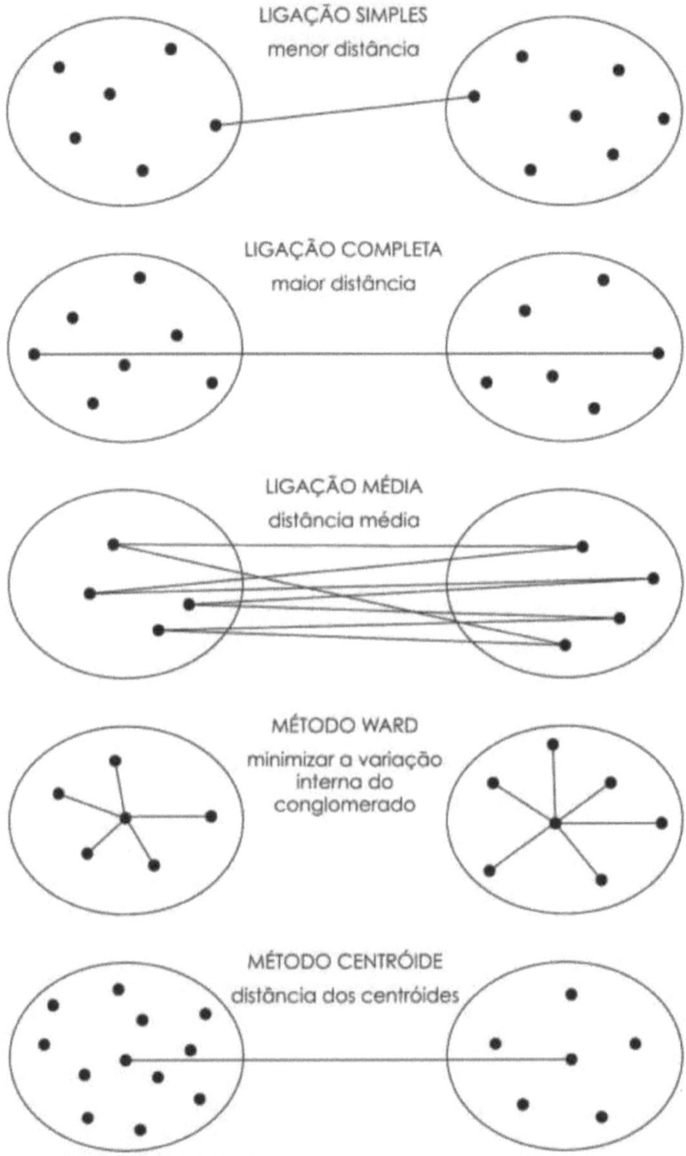

Figure 9 - Hierarchical clustering methods
Source: Aaker, Kumar and Day (2010)

Once the method to be used has been defined, it is also necessary to choose the linking method, the most commonly used of which are the simple, complete and average links, the Ward method and the centroid. **Figure 9** illustrates these different methods.

The simple linkage procedure is based on the shortest distance. It finds the two individuals separated by the shortest distance and places them in the first group. Then the next smallest distance is found and the third individual is brought together with the first two to form a group, or a new two-member group is formed. The process continues until all the individuals are in a group. This procedure is also known as the nearest neighbour approach.

The complete linkage procedure is similar to the simple linkage, only the grouping criterion is now the greatest distance. For this reason, it is also called the farthest neighbour approach.

The average linkage method starts in the same way as the previous ones, but the clustering criterion is the average distance between the individuals in one cluster and the individuals in another cluster.

The Ward method is based on the loss of information resulting from the grouping of individuals into conglomerates, measured by the total sum of the squares of the deviations of each individual in relation to the average of the conglomerate in which the object was inserted.

In the centroid method, the distance between groups is the distance between their centroids. The centroid is the point whose coordinates are the averages of all the observations in the cluster.

In this thesis, we opted for the Ward linkage method because it tends to form clusters of similar sizes and thus makes it easier to choose the number of clusters to consider.

Once all the previous steps had been completed, as described above, the next step was to carry out the procedure to obtain the clusters, still using the statistical software

Minitab 17, with the following driving variables: average IT spending (MG), average relative profit (ML); Factor 1 PS - perception of new products and services; Factor 2 AP - perception of increased productivity; Factor 3 RC - perception of reduced costs.

At this point a central question arises in cluster analysis: how to determine the final number of groups to be formed. According to the theory on the subject, there is no objective standard procedure for selection, especially since there is no internal statistical criterion used for inference, such as statistical significance tests for other multivariate methods. Researchers make use of various methods to aid the decision, the so-called stopping rules, but in the end it is up to the researcher to complement the strictly empirical judgement with any conceptual and theoretical aspects about the relationships studied that may suggest a natural number of groups (Hair et al., 2010; Corrar, Paulo and Dias Filho, 2009, Fávero et al., 2009).

A widely used stopping rule is the analysis of the measure called the distance between centroids, in which the greater the distance, the more heterogeneous the groupings are, which is one of the criteria that is sought when using the cluster analysis technique, as described above (Romesburg, 1990).

Another important element to help determine the number of clusters and define their elements is the graphical representation, which is called a dendogram or phenogram.

While carrying out the procedures to define the clusters, with the help of Minitab 17 statistical software, we arrived, after several analyses, at four clusters, as shown in the dendogram in **Graph 4**.

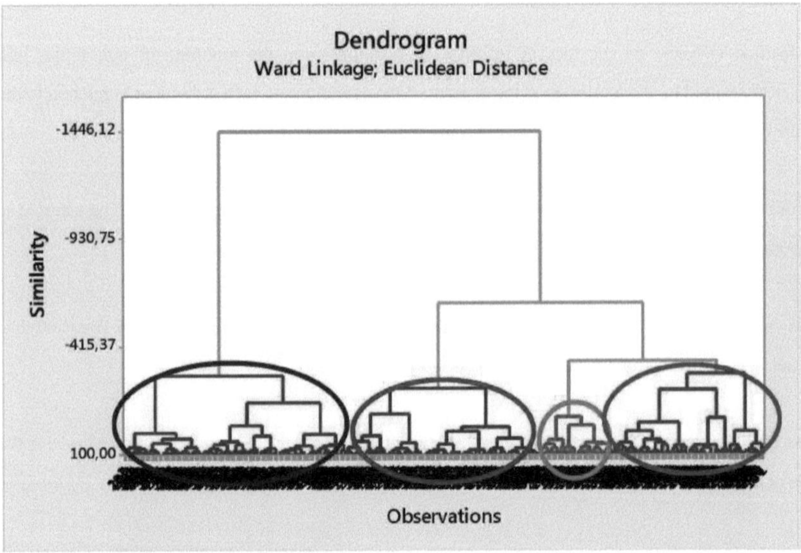

Graph 4 - Dendogram - four *clusters*
Source: Prepared by the author using Minitab 17 statistical software.

The final stage of the cluster analysis technique consists of validating, describing and interpreting the groupings, which is done by comparing the profiles of the individuals. Furthermore, as the theory on the subject suggests, in order to study the differences between groups, it is best to use the variables in their original form, i.e. without taking into account the factors and standardisation carried out.

To describe the groups, variables that were not considered in the grouping process are also used, the so-called discriminating variables: in our case, the company's sector of activity, average number of employees, average annual net revenue, length of time the company has been using IT, managers' perception of the strategic impact of IT in the future (IE) and managers' perception of the impact of legal changes on IT spending and investment (IF).

The use of distribution graphs is extremely useful for analysing the differences between groups, and the analysis of profiles often allows us to name each of the groups obtained appropriately, which makes it easier to communicate the results.

We will present these procedures in the following section on presenting and analysing the results.

When you apply the cluster analysis technique to classify a set of individuals, you hope to obtain a solution that is logical, i.e. that can be interpreted in the context of the problem you are studying. This interpretation requires analysis by an expert in the field.

CHAPTER 5

Presentation and analysis of results

The 355 companies that make up the final sample are divided into sectors of activity as follows: 30 per cent commerce, 31 per cent industry and 39 per cent services, as shown in **Graph 5**. **Table 6** shows the characteristics of these companies according to the information collected.

Graph 5 - Sector of activity - 355 companies in the final sample
Source: Prepared by the author

Table 6 - Characteristics of the companies in the final sample

Indicator	Complete Sample	Trade	Industry	Services
Number of companies	355	108	110	137
How long have you been using IT (average age)	9,1	7.8	10.5	9,0
Average number of employees over the last 3 years	131	33	272	94
Average of the last 3 years of keyboards in use	58	19	97	57
Average revenue over the last 3 years (in millions of reais)	60.896	24.587	114.496	46.483
Average of the last 3 years of hiccups (% of revenue)	11,113%	11.77%	10,68%	18,51%
Average IT spending over the last 3 years (% of revenue)	2.41%	1.58%	133%	3,93%
Impact of IT today on cost reduction (HRC)	3.22	3.11	3.31	3,24
The impact of IT today on increasing productivity (HAP)	3.38	3.39	3.23	3,49
Impact of IT today on products and services (HPS)	3.04	2.99	2.80	3,26
Impact of U in the future on cost reduction (FRC)	3.52	3.44	3.65	3,48
Impact of U in the future on increased productivity (FAP)	3.56	3.54	3.53	3,61
Future impact of U on products and services (FPS)	3.35	3.33	3.20	3,47
Average impact - considering the 6 variables	3.34	3.30	3.29	3,43
IT's strategic impact on the future (IE)	3.18	3.16	3.15	3,23
Impact of legal changes	3.29	3.31	3.45	3,15

Source: Developed by the author

As mentioned above, the process of developing the *cluster* analysis described above, using Minitab 17 statistical *software*, resulted in the sample being classified into four distinct groups of companies, the result of which is shown in **Table 7**, where the percentages take into account the calculation by column/cluster.

Table 7 - *Cluster* characteristics

	Sample	Cluster 1	Cluster 2	Cluster 3	Cluster 4
Name	Complete	Digital	Prudent	Conservatives	Analogue
Sector - Trade	**30%**	15%	47%	24%	34%
Sector - Industry	**31%**	11%	43%	59%	32%
Sector - Services	**39%**	74%	9%	17%	34%
How long have you been using IT (average age)	**9,1**	8,7	9,0	10,2	9,3
Average number of employees over the last 3 years	**131**	82	137	196	162
Average of the last 3 years of keyboards in use	**58**	51	50	85	64
Average revenue over the last 3 years (in millions of reais)	**60.896**	45.076	59.643	128.890	52.554
Average profitability over the last 3 years (% of revenue)	**14,03%**	21,92%	11,75%	9,16%	7,82%
Average IT spending over the last 3 years (% of revenue)	**2,41%**	4,65%	0,94%	1,30%	1,54%
Impact of IT today on cost reduction (HRC)	**3,22**	3,59	3,58	3,34	2,18
Impact of IT today on increasing productivity (HAP)	**3,38**	3,84	3,78	2,46	2,65
Impact of IT today on products and services (HPS)	**3,04**	3,56	3,20	3,07	2,06
Future impact of IT on cost reduction (FRC)	**3,52**	3,80	3,94	3,49	2,60
Future impact of IT on productivity growth (FAP)	**3,56**	3,94	3,98	2,80	2,86
Future impact of IT on products and services (FPS)	**3,35**	3,77	3,62	3,29	2,41
Average impact - considering the 6 variables	3,34	3,75	3,69	3,08	2,46
IT's strategic impact on the future (IE)	**3,18**	3,55	3,36	3,00	2,52
Impact of legal changes	**3,29**	3,15	3,48	3,27	3,27

Source: Developed by the author
Note: The managers' perceptions were calculated using the average, considering 1 for DT: totally disagree, 2 for DP: partially disagree, 3 for CP: partially agree and 4 for CT: totally agree. Therefore, this categorical variable was treated quantitatively.

Inspired by the **"Magic Quadrant", Figure 10** shows a snapshot of the four groupings and their respective results.

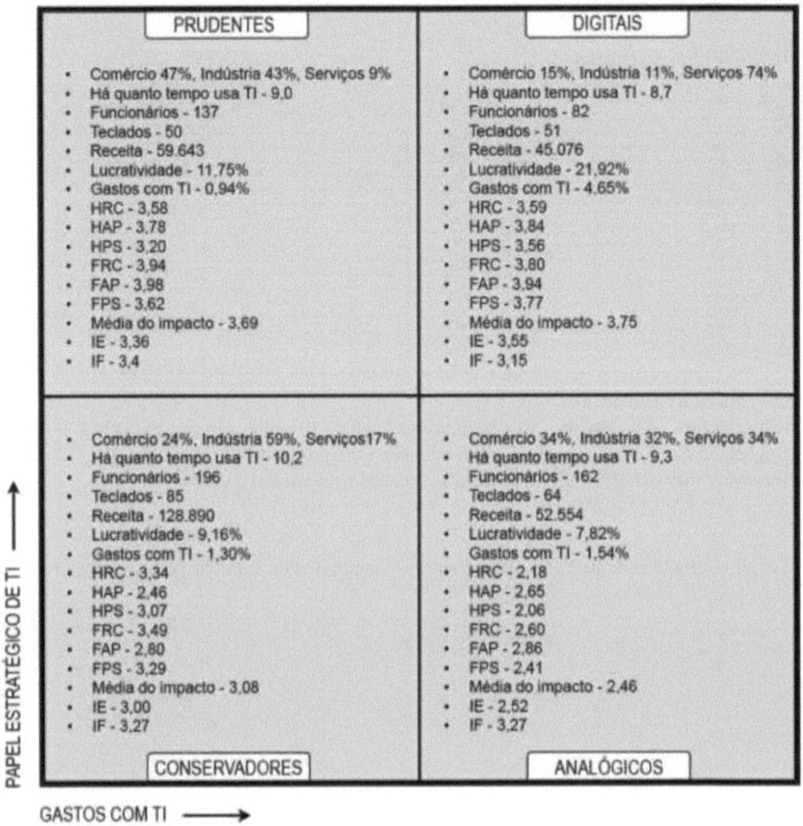

Figure 10 - IT role and IT spending

Source: Prepared by the author

Cluster 1, dubbed "Digital", is mostly made up of companies in the service sector, whose managers perceive IT as playing a strategic role in the company today and in the future in all the aspects analysed. Consistent with this perception, these companies spend the most on IT and, as a result, they achieve high net annual profitability. Compared to the entire sample, the "Digitals" spend almost twice as much on IT and achieve 56 per cent higher profitability than the sample average.

Cluster 2, dubbed "Prudent", *is* mostly made up of companies in the commerce and industry sectors, whose managers see IT playing a strategic role in the company today and in the future in all the aspects analysed, but to a lesser extent than the "Digitals". On the other hand, these companies spend the least on IT and their net annual profitability is higher than that of the companies in clusters 3 and 4, but below the profitability of the "Digitals". The "Prudent" spend 39 per cent more on IT than the average for the entire sample and manage to achieve 83 per cent of the average net annual profitability for the entire sample.

Cluster 3, dubbed "Conservatives", is mostly made up of companies in the industrial sector, with a larger number of employees and higher annual revenues, whose managers see IT playing a discreetly strategic role in the company today and in the future in all the aspects analysed, except for increased productivity. These companies also spend less on IT, being ahead in spending only of the "Prudents"; however, their net annual profitability is below that achieved by the "Prudents", being slightly higher only in comparison to the companies in cluster 4. The average IT spending of the "Conservatives" is approximately half the average of the entire sample and they manage to achieve 65% of the average net annual profitability of the entire sample.

Cluster 4, called "Analogues", also includes companies from all three sectors. The managers in this group perceive IT as playing a non-strategic role in the company today and in the future, in all the aspects analysed, they spend less on IT than the "Digitals", but they spend more on IT than the "Prudents" and "Conservatives"; as far as net annual profitability is concerned, it is the lowest of all four groups. Analogues" spend 64% more on IT than the average for the whole sample and achieve approximately half the average net annual profitability of the whole sample.

As already mentioned, the use of distribution graphs is extremely useful for analysing both the differences between the groupings and the profiles that made it possible to baptise each of the groups obtained, shown in Table 7. Below are the distribution and analysis graphs for each of the variables used.

Sector of activity

As can be seen from the analysis of **Graph 6,** cluster 1, "Digital", is mainly made up of companies from the service sector; cluster 2, "Prudent", is mostly made up of companies from the commercial and industrial sectors; cluster 3, "Conservative", is predominantly made up of companies from the industrial sector; and cluster 4, "Analogue", is made up of companies from all three sectors of activity in equal measure.

Graph 6 - Sector of activity by *cluster*

Source: Prepared by the author

<u>How long has the company been using IT</u>

As we can see from the analysis of **Graph 7**, with regard to the length of time the company has been using IT, we were unable to see any significant differences in behaviour between the companies in each of the groupings, which leads us to conclude that this aspect does not play a major role in defining their profile.

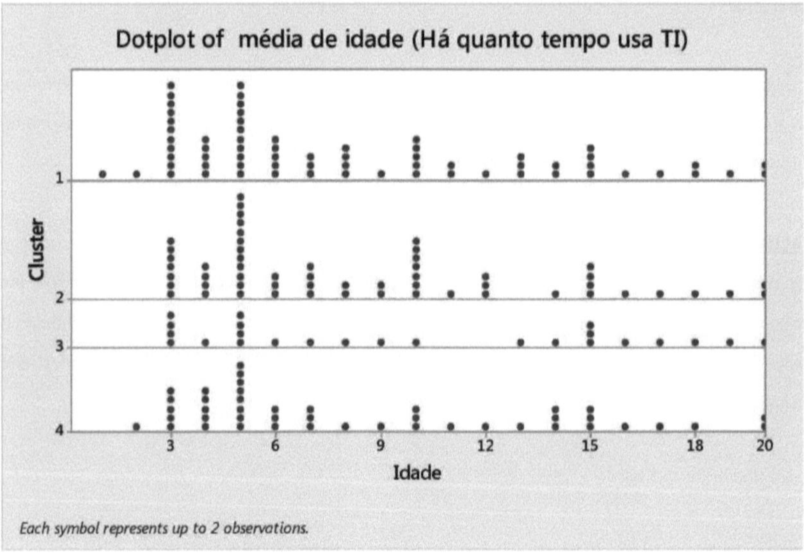

Graph 7 - Average age by *cluster*

Source: Prepared by the author using Minitab 17 statistical software.

Number of employees

As you can see in **Graph 8,** cluster 1, "Digital", is made up of a majority of smaller companies, which leads it to have an average of 82 employees, significantly lower than the average of the other three clusters; followed by cluster 2, "Prudent", with an average of 137 employees; and cluster 4, "Analogue", with 162 employees; while cluster 3, "Conservative", with the fewest companies with few employees, has the highest average, reaching 196 employees.

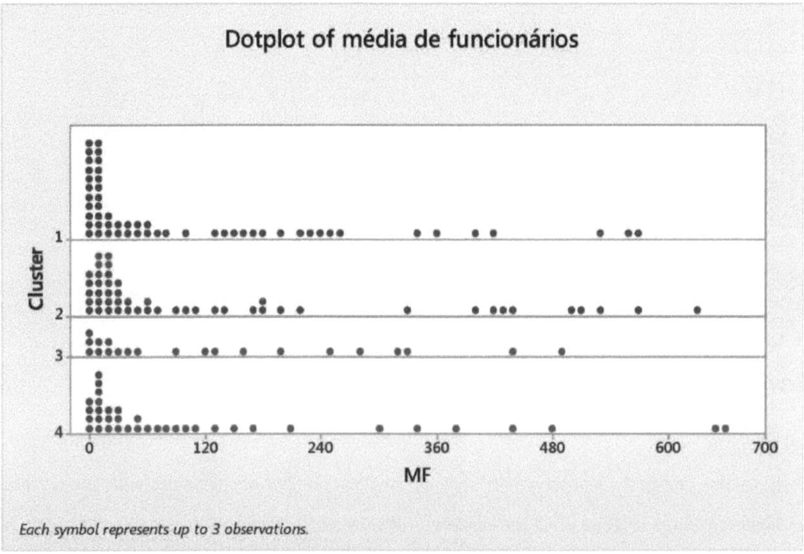

Graph 8 - Average number of employees per *cluster*

Source: Prepared by the author using Minitab 17 statistical software.

Number of keyboards in use

Graph 9 shows that cluster 1, "Digital", and cluster 2, "Prudent", have a similar distribution and consequently have a very close average, with 51 and 50 keyboards in use respectively, while cluster 4, "Analogue", which, despite having a similar distribution to the first two, has fewer companies with a smaller number of keyboards in use, therefore has an average around 30% higher than the previous clusters, reaching 64 keyboards; Cluster 3, "Conservatives", with fewer companies with few keyboards and a higher proportional number of companies with more keyboards in use, has the highest average, reaching 85 keyboards.

It's interesting to analyse that in the ratio between the average number of keyboards in use and the number of employees, cluster 1, "Digital", has an index of 62%, much higher than the other clusters, which are between 36% and 43%. This finding may suggest that the considerable higher volume of spending by the "Digitals" is also reflected in the greater number of keyboards, which may mean greater digital inclusion within the company.

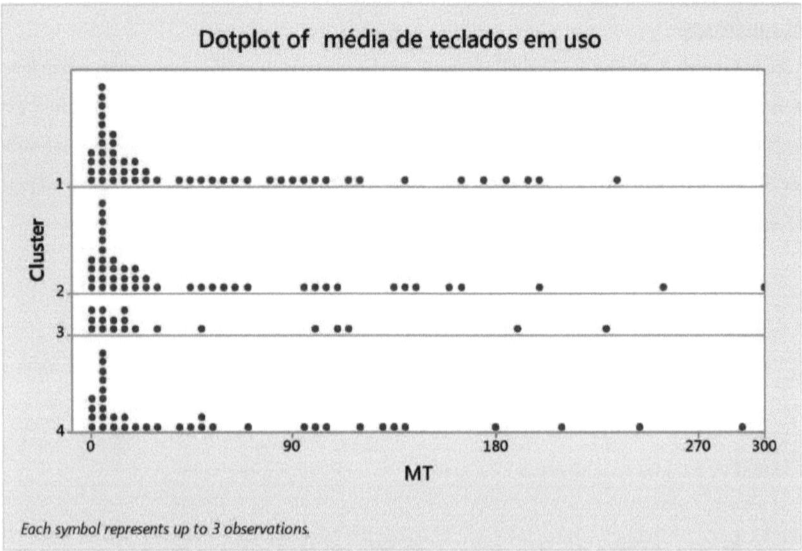

Graph 9 - Average number of keyboards in use

Source: Prepared by the author using Minitab 17 statistical software.

Net annual revenue

Graph 10 shows that cluster 3, "Conservatives", has the smallest number of companies with low revenue, and thus the highest average revenue of all the clusters, at R$129 million, which is also compatible with the highest number of employees.

Cluster 1, "Digital", despite having some companies with higher average annual revenues, also has a higher concentration of companies with low average annual revenues, which leads it to have the lowest value, totalling around R$45 million.

Cluster 2, "Prudentes", which has a similar concentration to cluster 4, "Analogues", due to the fact that it has some companies with a higher average than the other cluster, reaches an average of around R$59 million, while the "Analogues" reach an average of around R$52 million.

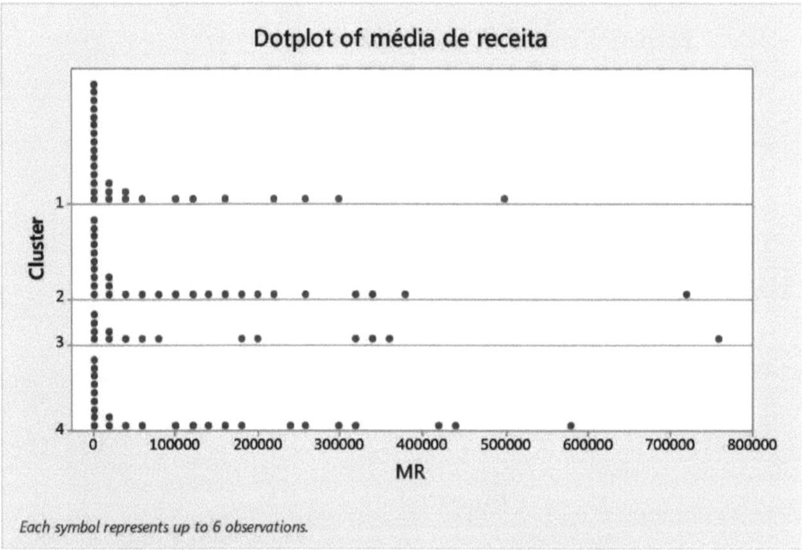

Graph 10 - Average annual net revenue

Source: Prepared by the author using Minitab 17 statistical software.

<u>Annual profitability</u>

Graph 11 shows that cluster 1, "Digital", has a large number of companies with high profitability (above 24%), and thus has the highest average of all the clusters, reaching 21.92%, a level approximately twice as high as that of the runner-up, "Prudent", and almost three times as high as that reached by "Analogue".

Cluster 2, "Prudentes", shows a distribution with several companies achieving profitability of between 12 per cent and 24 per cent, which puts them in second place with an average profitability of 11.75 per cent.

The "Conservatives" and "Analogues" have a similar distribution, with companies reaching an average profitability of no more than 23%; however, like the "Analogues", they have a much higher concentration of companies with low profitability and come last in this regard, reaching an average of 7.82%, behind the "Conservatives", with an average profitability of 9.16%.

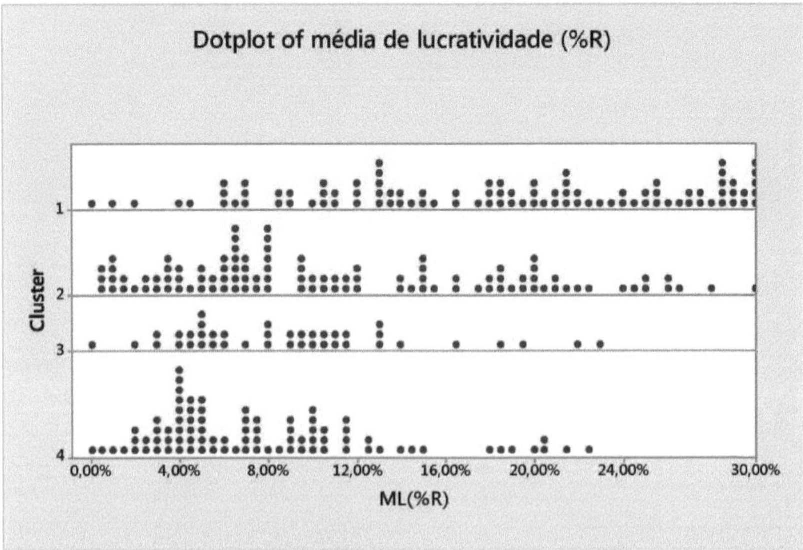

Graph 11 - Average annual profitability

Source: Prepared by the author using Minitab 17 statistical software.

Total IT spend

As we can see in **Graph 12**, the "Digitals" show a very different behaviour in terms of total IT spending compared to the other groupings, spending more than 3 times the amount spent by the "Analogues", more than 3.5 times the amount spent by the "Conservatives" and almost 5 times the total spent by the "Prudents"; reaching a rate of 4.65% of their net revenue.

The "Analogues", in second place in this indicator, have a similar distribution to the "Prudents" and "Conservatives", except for the fact that several companies achieve rates above 5%, while in the other two groupings this doesn't happen, which is why the "Analogues" achieve an average of 1.54% of revenue.

The "Conservatives" and the "Prudents" also behave very similarly in this respect, with the former averaging 1.30 per cent of their revenue, while the latter, who have the lowest average IT spending, only reach 0.94 per cent of their revenue.

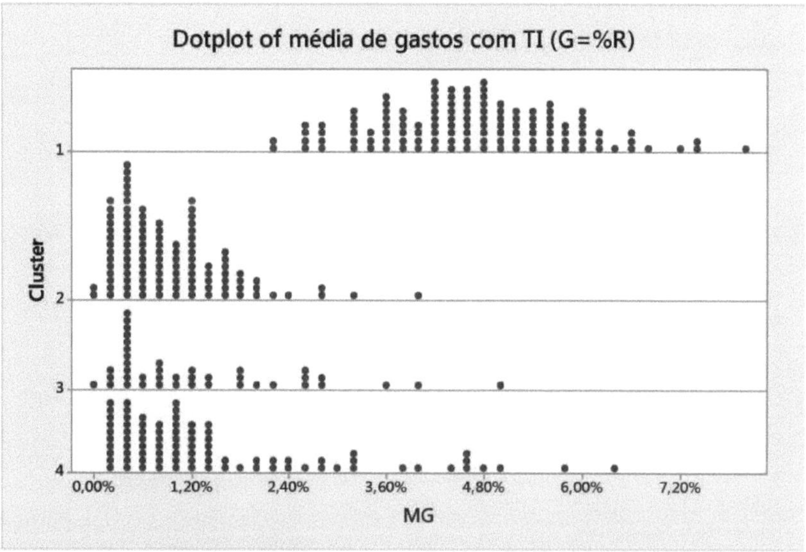

Graph 12 - Average IT spending

Source: Prepared by the author using Minitab 17 statistical software.

<u>Impact of IT today on cost reduction</u>

Analysing **Graph 13** shows that the "Digitals" and the "Prudents" have a very close perception of the impact that IT has on reducing costs today. On a scale of the degree of agreement about the contribution ranging from 1 to 4, they reached an average of 3.59 and 3.58 respectively, which indicates great importance.

The "Conservatives" also attach importance to this aspect, but to a lesser extent than the other two groupings above, and within the same scale they reached an average of 3.34.

As for the "Analogues", IT does not have the same relevance for reducing costs today. With several companies having a low degree of agreement about the contribution, the grouping reaches an average of 2.18, which, within the scale used, means disagreement about the contribution.

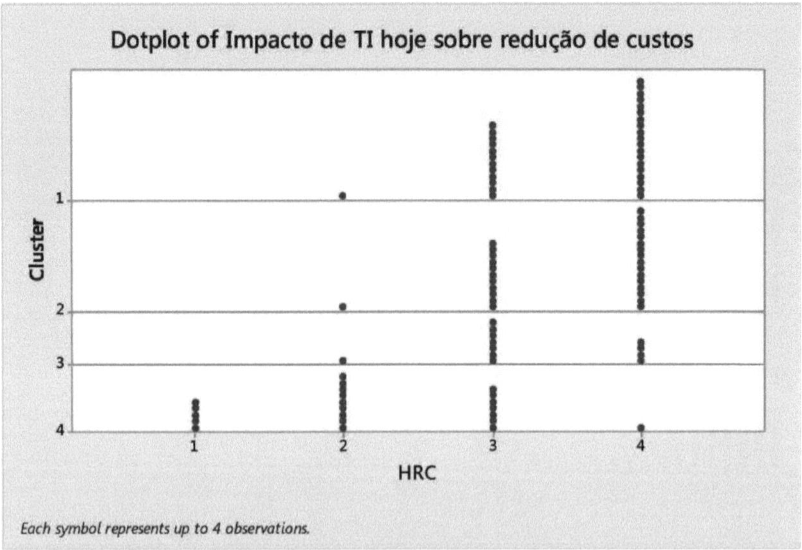

Graph 13 - Impact of IT today on cost reduction
Source: Prepared by the author using Minitab 17 statistical software.

<u>The impact of IT today on increasing productivity</u>

As can be seen by analysing **Graph 14**, as with the cost reduction aspect, the "Digitals" and the "Prudents" have a very close perception of the impact that IT has on increasing productivity in the present. On a scale of degree of agreement about the contribution ranging from 1 to 4, they reached an average of 3.84 and 3.78 respectively, which indicates great importance.

As for the "Analogues" and "Conservatives", IT does not have the same relevance for increasing productivity in the present, with several companies having a low degree of agreement about the contribution: the "Analogues" reach an average of 2.65 and the "Conservatives" reach the lowest average of 2.46, which, within the scale used, means disagreement about the contribution.

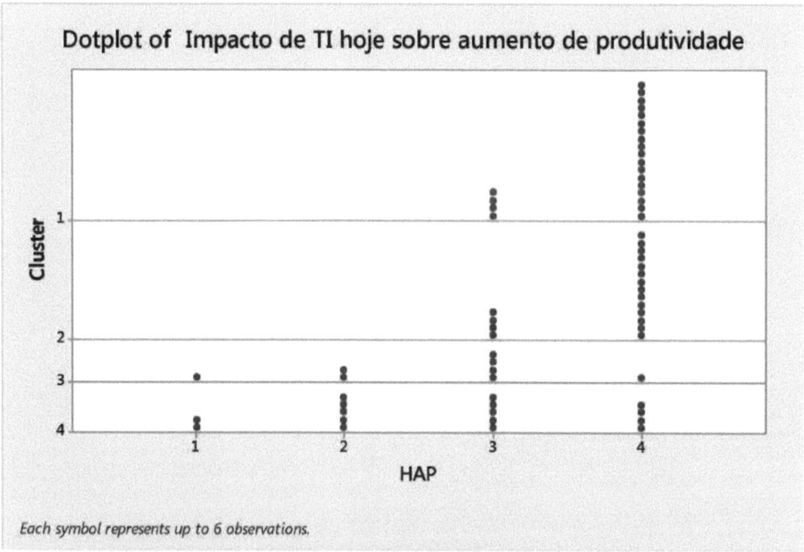

Graph 14 - Impact of IT today on increased productivity
Source: Prepared by the author using Minitab 17 statistical software.

<u>**Impact of IT today on new products and services**</u>

Graph 15 shows that the "Digitals" perceive the impact of IT on new products and services in the present more intensely than the other groupings, reaching the highest average of 3.56, which indicates great importance in this regard.

Next, we find the "Prudent" and "Conservative" with very similar patterns of perception on the issue, with averages of 3.20 and 3.07 respectively, which also means some importance.

Again for the "Analogues", as in the previous questions, IT does not have the same relevance for new products and services today. With a high number of companies with a low degree of agreement about the contribution, the grouping reaches the lowest average of 2.06, which, within the scale used, means disagreement about the contribution.

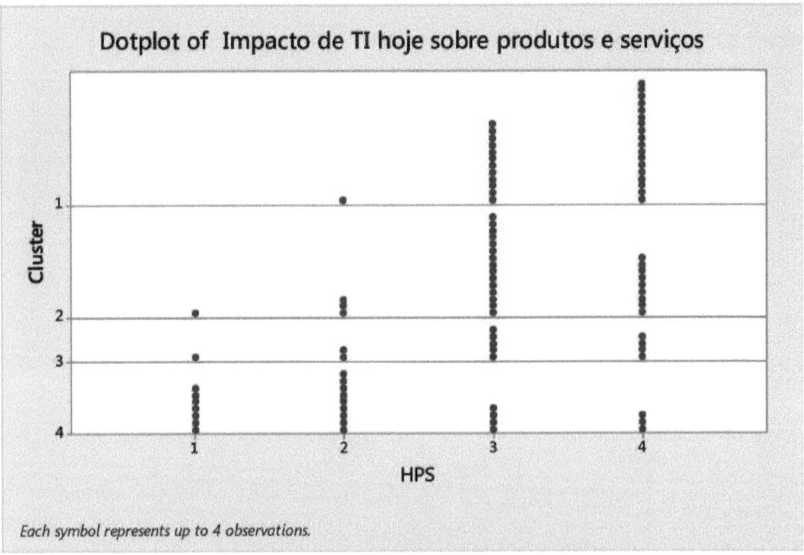

Graph 15 - Impact of IT today on new products and services
Source: Prepared by the author using Minitab 17 statistical software.

Impact of future IT on cost reduction

Analysis of **Graph 16** shows a very similar behaviour to that of all the groupings with regard to the perception of the impact of cost reductions in the present, but with a rise towards greater importance in the intensity of perceptions.

So we see that the "Digitals" and the "Prudents" have a very close perception of the impact that IT could have on reducing costs in the future. On a scale of the degree of agreement about the contribution ranging from 1 to 4, they reached an average of 3.80 and 3.94 respectively, which denotes great importance.

It is interesting to note that the "Prudent" seem to perceive a more intense impact of IT contributions in the future than in the present, both in this aspect of cost reduction and in the following aspects of increased productivity and new products and services.

The "Conservatives" attach importance to this aspect, but to a lesser extent than the other two groupings above, and within the same scale they reached an average of 3.49.

As for the "Analogues", IT is not as relevant to reducing costs in the future. With several companies having a low degree of agreement about the contribution, the grouping reaches an average of 2.60, which, within the scale used, means disagreement about the contribution.

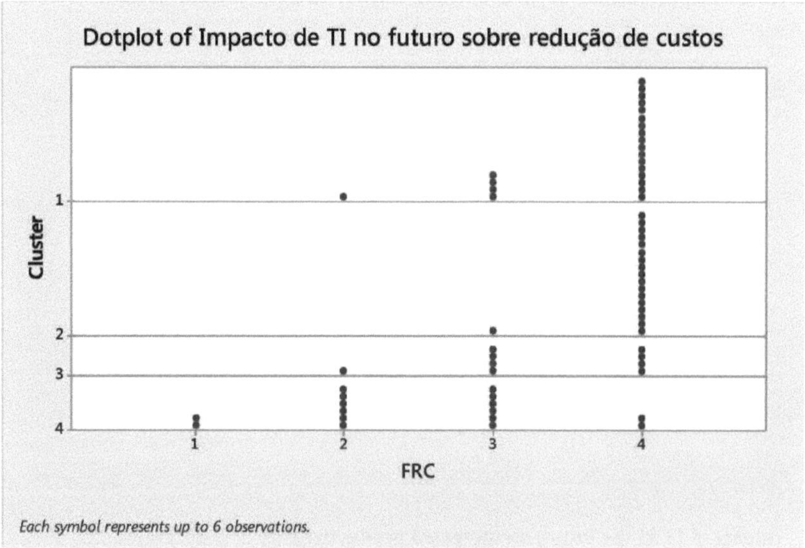

Graph 16 - Impact of IT in the future on cost reduction

Source: Prepared by the author using Minitab 17 statistical software.

Impact of future IT on increasing productivity

Graph 17 again shows very similar behaviour to that of the "Digitals" and "Prudents", now with regard to the perception of the impact that IT could have on increasing productivity in the future, also with a rise towards greater importance in the intensity of perceptions.

The "Digitals" and the "Prudents", on the same scale of the degree of agreement on the contribution ranging from 1 to 4, reached an average of 3.94 and 3.98 respectively, which indicates great importance. It's also interesting to note that, once again, the "Prudents" have the strongest perception of the impact of IT in the future than all the other groupings.

Again, for the "Analogues" and the "Conservatives", IT does not have the same relevance for increasing productivity in the future. With several companies having a low degree of agreement about the contribution, the "Analogues" reach an average of 2.86 and the "Conservatives" reach the lowest average of 2.80, which, within the scale used, means disagreement about the contribution.

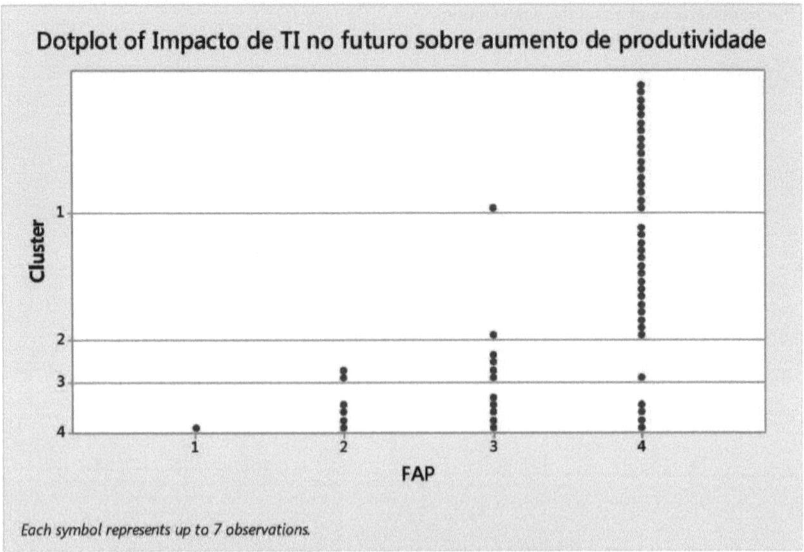

Graph 17 - Impact of IT in the future on increased productivity
Source: Prepared by the author using Minitab 17 statistical software.

Future impact of IT on new products and services

Graph 18 shows that the "Digitals" perceive the impact of IT on new products and services in the future more intensely than the other groupings, reaching the highest average of 3.77, which indicates great importance in this regard.

With a similar pattern, but less intense, we find the "Prudent", with an average of 3.62, which also indicates great importance in this aspect.

Next come the "Conservatives", who attach some importance to the aspect, demonstrated by the average of 3.29.

And lastly, the "Analogues", who reached the lowest average of 2.41, quite consistently across all aspects, showing that managers do not perceive the importance of IT in the pursuit of the benefits pointed out; in this case, on the impact of IT in the future on new products and services.

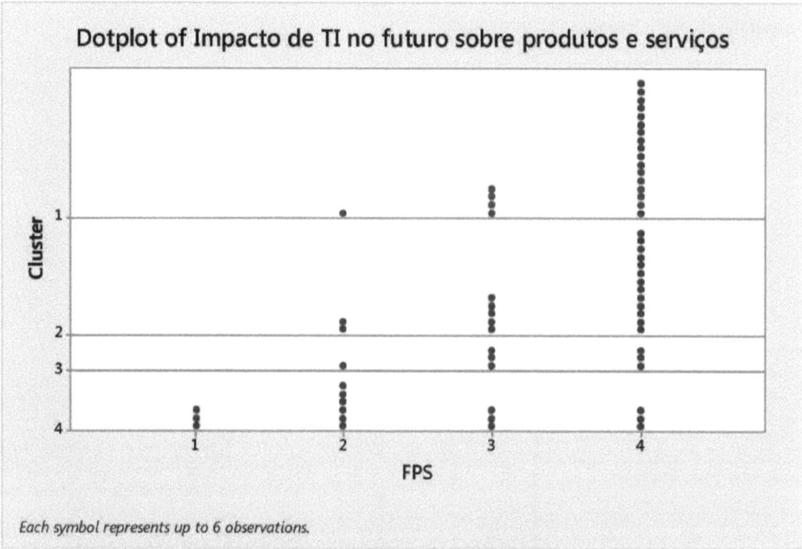

Graph 18 - Future impact of IT on new products and services
Source: Prepared by the author using Minitab 17 statistical software.

<u>**IT's strategic impact on business in the future**</u>

In this question, the intention was, in a way, to confirm or not what had been observed about the impact of IT in the future, but assessing the perception in a way that was more linked to the company's performance as a whole.

Graph 19 shows confirmation of the behaviour of each of the groupings in a similar way to that presented for the perceptions of each aspect in isolation.

Thus, the "Digitals" perceive the strategic impact of IT in the future more intensely than the other groupings, reaching the highest average of 3.55, denoting great importance.

With a similar pattern, but less intense, we find the "Prudent", with an average of 3.36, which also denotes great importance. Next come the "Conservatives", who attach some importance to the aspect, demonstrated by the average of 3.00.

And finally, the "Analogues" reached the lowest average of 2.52, always quite consistently throughout all the aspects, showing that managers do not perceive the importance of IT in the pursuit of the benefits pointed out;

in this case, about the strategic impact of IT in the future.

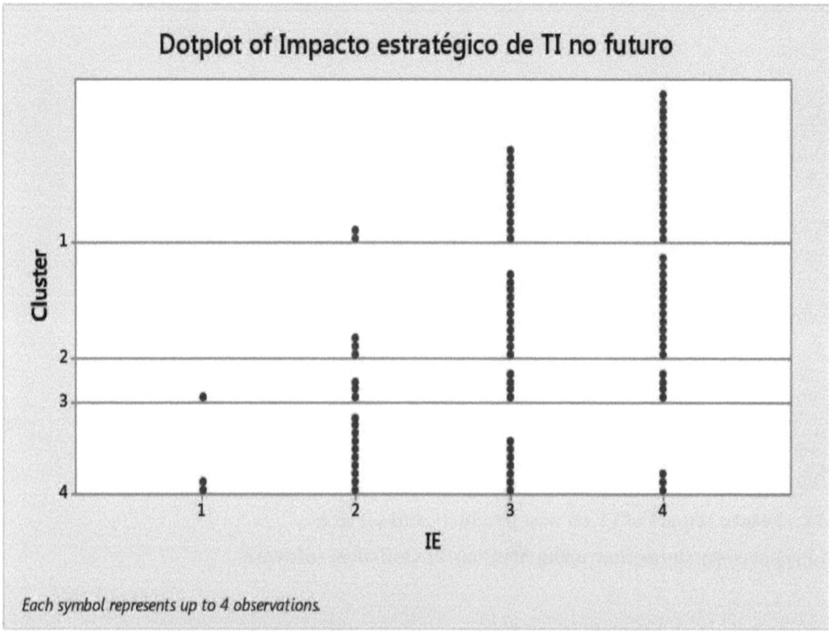

Graph 19 - Strategic impact of IT in the future

Source: Prepared by the author using Minitab 17 statistical software.

Impact of legal changes on IT spending and investment

As we can see from the analysis of **Graph 20**, with regard to the impact of legal changes requiring companies to submit their tax obligations digitally on IT spending and investment, we were unable to discern any significant differences in behaviour between the companies in each of the groupings, which leads us to conclude that this aspect does not play a major role in defining their profile.

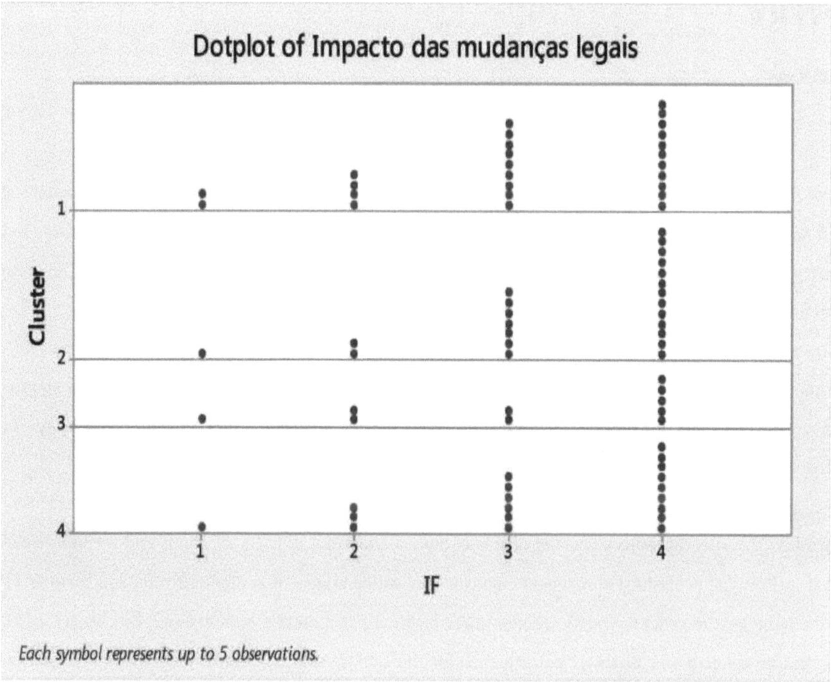

Graph 20 - Impact of legal changes

Source: Prepared by the author using Minitab 17 statistical software.

CHAPTER 6

Conclusions

This research sought to investigate the impact of IT spending and investment on the financial performance of small and medium-sized Brazilian companies. And, in this context, it also sought to investigate whether (and how) managers' perceptions of the stages of computerisation and the role IT plays in the company have an impact on these results.

The general aim of this thesis was to see if there is an association between IT spending and investment and the performance of small and medium-sized companies, mediated by managers' perceptions of the stages of computerisation and the role IT plays in the company.

With regard to the specific objectives, the aim was both to map out clusters of small and medium-sized companies in Portugal according to managers' perceptions of the stages of computerisation and the role IT plays in the company, in order to clarify whether there is any distinct pattern of behaviour, by clusters, of IT spending and investment and financial performance for the sample studied, and to identify the association between IT spending and investment and annual net profit in the period studied.

These objectives were fully achieved as the results found and analysed in the previous section point to evidence of a positive association between IT spending and investment and increased company profitability, especially given the presence of managers' specific perceptions of the role IT plays in the company.

This work contributes to a better understanding of the subject and presents the following conclusions:

1) The greater the managers' perception of the positive impact of IT on the company's business processes as a whole, enabling the company to achieve benefits in terms of cost reduction, increased productivity and new products and services, the greater the impact of IT spending and investment on the company's profitability.

2) Companies with a higher level of spending and investment in IT, combined with a strong perception on the part of managers that IT can make a positive contribution to the company's objectives, in order to reduce costs, increase productivity and develop new products and services, result in a higher level of profitability, as was the case with the grouping known as "Digital".

3) Companies whose managers intensely perceive that IT cannot make a positive contribution to the company's objectives, in order to reduce costs, increase productivity and develop new products and services, even if they make above-average levels of spending and investment in IT, have a lower level of profitability, as was the case with the group called "Analogues".

4) Merely attributing the company's profitability results to the levels of IT spending and investment does not seem to be enough, as several previous studies have shown (Berndt and Morrison, 1995; Wolff, 1999; Triplett, 1999; Gordon, 2001).

5) Another interesting piece of evidence concerns companies whose managers have a strong perception that IT can make a positive contribution to the company's objectives, with the aim of reducing costs, increasing productivity and developing new products and services. Even though these companies maintain a level of spending and investment in IT that is below the average for other companies, they still end up showing above-average results in terms of profitability, as was the case with the group called "Prudentes".

6) The behaviour of the group known as "Conservatives" seems to confirm the evidence pointed out above, because, despite having higher levels of spending and investment in IT than the "Prudents", the fact that the managers of these companies perceive, in a less intense way, the contribution that IT can make to the company's objectives, in order to reduce costs, increase productivity and develop new products and services, ends up leading them to a lower level of profitability than the "Prudents", thus reinforcing the impact of the managers' perception of the role that IT plays in the company.

7) And similarly, although the "Conservatives" have lower levels of spending and investment in IT than the "Analogues", the fact that the managers of these companies perceive that IT can make a positive contribution to the company's objectives, unlike the managers of the "Analogues" group who perceive that IT cannot make a positive contribution to the company's objectives, leads them to a higher level of profitability than the "Analogues".

8) With regard to the length of time the company has been using IT and the stages of computerisation, this research fails to capture significant relationships with company performance.

9) As for the impact of the legal changes requiring companies to submit their tax obligations digitally on IT spending and investment, to varying degrees, the managers' perception is that this has led companies to increase the level of IT spending and investment.

10) With regard to the distribution of companies in the different sectors of activity, there seems to be evidence that the companies whose managers perceive the benefits that IT can bring to the company more intensely and jointly spend more on IT (the so-called "Digital" behaviour), there is a large predominance of companies in the service sector. While companies whose managers perceive the benefits that IT can bring to the company with some intensity, but don't spend much on IT ("Conservative" behaviour), there is a predominance of companies in the industrial sector.

The analysis of all the results presented can be seen in Figure 11 and Graph 21, which summarise the main conclusions relating to each of the clusters found in this research.

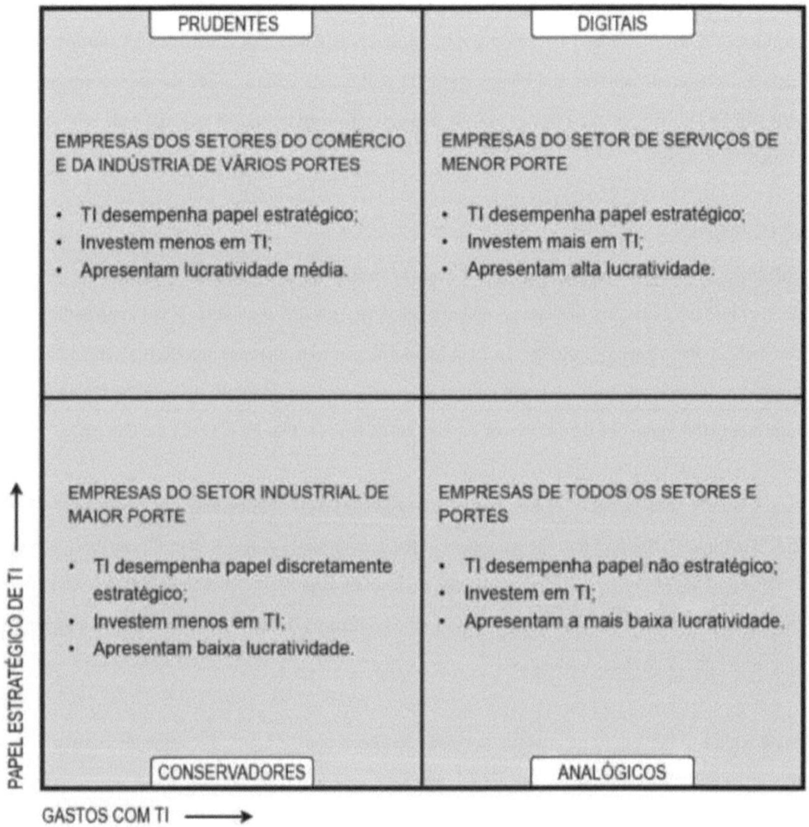

Figure 11 - *Cluster* overview

Source: Prepared by the author

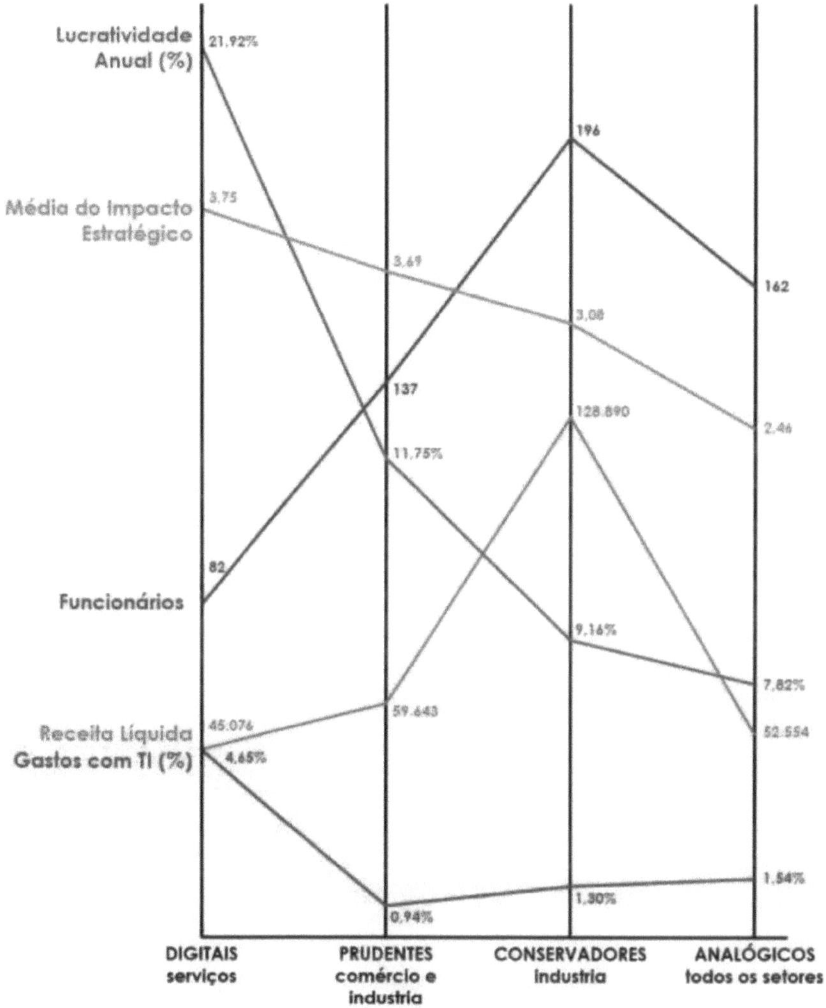

Graph 21 - ***Cluster*** **behaviour**

Source: Prepared by the author

This thesis makes important theoretical and practical contributions, covering both the academic and managerial spheres, helping to develop a better understanding of various aspects, especially when we consider the small number of studies on the relationship between IT and business performance in the context of small and medium-sized Brazilian companies.

From a theoretical point of view, firstly with regard to business performance, a construct that still lacks greater agreement among researchers, this study has yet another way of approaching it, which, despite considering financial indicators, as several previous studies have done (Johnston, Wade and McClean, 2007; Mithas et al., 2012; Gomez and Pather, 2012; Mustafa, 2015), as a novelty includes the perception of managers about the impact and benefits of using IT, as found in the work of Lefebvre, Mason and Lefebvre (1997).

Another significant contribution to the academic field is with regard to understanding aspects relating to the use of IT and the impact of its benefits on small and medium-sized Brazilian companies, as not many studies were found in the literature researched, except for Gonçalves (1994), Prates and Ospina (2004) and Lunardi, Dolci and Maçada (2010).

Also with regard to theories on perceptions of the stages of computerisation and the role of IT (Nolan, 1979; McFarlan, 1984; Nolan and MacFarlan, 2005), this research makes theoretical contributions as it further explores the concepts in the context of small and medium-sized Brazilian companies, as well as their relationship with company performance.

A further contribution in the field of theory concerns the use of the cluster analysis technique to explore contexts relating to IT, since this technique has wide practical application but is often not used for research in the area.

As a practical contribution, which is of more interest to company managers, this thesis helps them to better understand the importance of the perception of the role that IT plays in the business, not only alerting them to worry about the volumes of spending and investment in IT, but also inviting them to think more deeply about the role that IT should play in each context.

Another practical contribution of this work is to indicate aspects to be taken into account in order to assess the impacts of IT spending and investment more specifically, and thus contribute to company managers thinking of IT much more as a means of achieving their objectives than as an end in itself.

Although all the procedures recommended in the literature for this type of research were followed (Aaker, Kumar and Day, 2010; Hair et al., 2011), a limitation of this research is the convenience sample, which restricts generalisation.

Another limitation encountered in developing this thesis was the resistance of managers to revealing their companies' financial data, either because they considered it strategic or because they didn't know exactly.

Furthermore, as these are small and medium-sized companies, with no need to publicly disclose their results, this information was provided directly by the managers.

From this work emerge some possibilities for future research: a first option concerns a more in-depth investigation by sector of activity, which may bring important discoveries, given that the sectors show significant differences in behaviour and results, as demonstrated by the "Digitals", mainly from the services sector, and the "Conservatives", made up mainly of companies from the industrial sector.

Another possibility for future research is, in addition to capturing managers' perceptions of the impacts of using IT, to objectively measure these impacts with regard to the three dimensions of benefits adopted in this work: cost reduction, increased productivity and new products and services.

References

- Aaker, D. A., Kumar, V.; Day, G. S. (2010) "Marketing Research", Atlas, São Paulo.
- Agarwal, R.; Lucas, H. C. (2005) "The Information Systems identity crisis: focusing on high visibility and high-impact research", MIS Quarterly, Vol. 29, No. 3, pp. 381-398.
- Albarracín, E.; Erazo, S.; Palacios, F. (2014) "Influencia de las tecnologias de la información y comunicación en el rendimento de las micro, pequenas y medianas empresas colombianas", Managerial Studies, Vol. 30, pp355-364.
- Albertin, A. L. (2009) Administração de informática - funções e fatores críticos de sucesso, Atlas, São Paulo.
- Albertin, A. L. (2010) Comércio Eletrônico - Modelo, Aspectos e Contribuições de sua Aplicação, Atlas, São Paulo.
- Albertin, A. L.; Albertin, R.M.M. (2012) "Dimensions of Information Technology Use: A Diagnostic and Analysis Tool", Revista de Administração Pública, Vol. 46, pp. 125-151.
- Aral, S.; Weill, P. (2007) "IT assets, organisational capabilities, and firm performance: How resource allocations and organisational differences explain performance variation", Organisation Science, Vol. 18, n. 5, pp. 763-780.
- Arendt, L. (2008) " Barriers to ICT adoption in Smes: How to bridge the digital divide?", Journal of Systems and Information Technology, Vol. 10, No. 2, pp. 93-108.
- Baines, S. (1999) "Servicing the media: freelancing, teleworking and 'enterprising' careers", New

Technology, Work and Employment, Vol. 14, No. 1.

- Barros, M. V. G.; Nahas, M. V. (2001) "Risk behaviours, self-rated health and perceived stress among industrial workers", Revista de Saúde Pública, Vol. 35(6), pp.554-63.

- Bayo-Moriones, A.; Billón, M.; Lera-López, F. (2013) "Perceived performance effects of ICT in manufacturing SMEs", Industrial Management & Data Systems, Vol. 113, No. 1.

- Bemdt, E. R.; Morrison, C. J. (1995) "High-tech Capital Formation and Economic Performance inU.S. Manufacturing Industries: AnExploratory Analysis", Journal of Econometrics, Vol. 65, pp. 9-43.

- Bharadwaj, A. S., Bharadwaj, S. G.; Konsynski, B. R. (1999) "Information Technology Effects on Firm Performance as Measured by Tobin's q", Management Science, Vol. 45, No. 7, pp 1008-1024.

- Bhatt, G. D.; Grover, V. (2005) "Types of information technology capabilities and their role in competitive advantage: An empirical study", Journal of Management Information Systems, Vol. 22, No. 2, pp. 253-277.

- Brito, L. A. L. (2007) Desempenho Empresarial, FGV, São Paulo.

- Brito, L. A. L.; Vasconcelos, F. C. (2004) "A Heterogeneidade do Desempenho, suas Causas e o Conceito de Vantagem Competitiva", RAC - Revista de Administração Contemporânea, Special Edition, pp 107-129.

- Brynjolfsson, E.; Hitt, L. M. (1995) "Information technology as a factor of production: The role of differences among firms", Economics of Innovation and New Technology, Vol. 3(4), pp. 183-199.

- Brynjolfsson, E.; Hitt, L. M. (1996) "Paradox lost? Firm-level evidence on the returns to information systems spending", Management Science, Vol. 42(4), pp. 541-558.

- Brynjolfsson, E.; Hitt, L. M. (1998) "Beyond the productivity paradox", Communications of the ACM, Vol. 41(8), pp. 49-55.

- Brynjolfsson, E.; Hitt, L. M. (2000) "Beyond computation: information technology - organisational transformation and business performance", Journal of Economic Perspectives, Vol. 14(4), pp. 23-48.

- Brynjolfsson, E.; Yang, S. (1996) "Information technology and productivity: a review of the literature", Advances in Computers, Vol. 43(1), pp.179-214.

- Byrd, T. A.; Marshall, T. T. (1997) "Relating Information Technology Investment to Organisational Performance: a Causal Model Analysis", Omega International Journal of Management Science, Vol.25, No. 1, pp43-56.

- Buchanan, J. R.; Linowes, R. G. (1980) "Making Distributed Data Processing Work", Harvard Business Review, Vol. 58, No. 5, pp143-161.

- Bussab, W. O.; Miazaki, E. S.; Andrade, D. F. (1990) "Introduction to Cluster Analysis", 9th National Symposium on Probability and Statistics, IME-USP, São Paulo.

- Callahan, C. M., Gabriel, E. A.; Smith, R. E. (2009) "The Effects of Inter-Firm Cost Correlation, IT Investment, and Product Cost Accuracy on Production Decisions and Firm profitability", Journal of Information Systems, Vol. 23, No. 1, pp. 51-78.

- Cao, G. (2010) "A four-dimensional view of IT business value", Systems Research and Behavioral Science, Vol. 27, No. 3, pp. 267-284.

- Carneiro, J. M. T.; Dib, L. A. (2006) "Building a Better Measure of Business Performance", Paper presented at the XXX Encontro da ANPAD - Associação Nacional de Pós-Graduação e Pesquisa em Administração, Salvador, Brazil.

- Ceolin, D. S. (2006) "O Conflito de Agência Exposto ao Efeito de Mercado: Um Estudo Empírico de Precificação de Ações da Bombril S/A", Master's thesis, Methodist University of São Paulo.

- Chakravarthy, B. S. (1986) "Measuring Strategic Performance", Strategic Management Journal, Vol.7, No. 5; ABI/INFORM Global, pp 437.

- Chinomona, R. (2013) "The fostering role of information technology on SME's strategic purchasing, logistics integration and business performance", Southern African Business Review, Vol. 17, No. 1, pp.76-97.

- Collis, J.; Hussey, R. (2005) "Research in Administration". Porto Alegre: Bookman.

- Consoli, D. (2012) "Literature analysis on determinant factors and the impact of ICT in SMEs", Procedia - Social and Behavioural Sciences, Vol. 62, pp93-97.

- Coppeland, T.; Koller, T.; Murrin, J. (2004) Valuation: Calculating and Managing the Value of Companies, Translated by Allan Vidigal Hastings, Makron Books, São Paulo.

- Corrar, L. J.; Paulo, E.; Dias Filho, J. M. (2009) Multivariate Analysis, Atlas, São Paulo.

- Creswell, J.W. (2009) "Research design: qualitative, quantitative, and mixed methods approaches". Los Angeles. SAGE Publications, Inc.

- De Haes, S.; Grembergen, W. V. (2009) "An Exploratory Study into IT Governance Implementations and its Impact on Business/IT Alignment", Information Systems Management, Vol. 26, pp. 123-137.

- Dehning, B.; Richardson, V. J. (2002) "Returns on investments in information technology: A research synthesis", Journal of Information Systems, Vol. 16(1), pp. 7-30.

- Devaraj, S.; Kohli, R. (2003) "Performance Impacts of Information Technology: Is Actual Usage the Missing Link?", Management Science, Vol. 49, n. 3, pp. 273-289.

- Devos, J.; Landeghem, H. V.; Deschoolmeester, D. (2008) "Outsourced Information Systems Failures in SMEs: a Multiple Case Study", The Electronic Journal Information Systems Evaluation, Vol. 11, No. 2, pp 73 - 82.

- Devos, J.; Landeghem, H. V.; Deschoolmeester, D. (2012) "Rethinking IT governance for SMEs", Industrial Management & Data Systems, Vol. 112, No. 2.

- Dewan, S.; Ren, F. (2011) "Information technology and firm boundaries: Impact on firm risk and retum performance", Information Systems Research, Vol. 22, No. 2, pp.369-388.

- Dewan, S.; Shi, C.; Gurbaxani, V. (2007) "Investigating the risk-return relationship of information technology investment: firm-level empirical analysis", Management Science, Vol. 53, No. 12, pp. 1829-1842.

- Dierckx, M. A.; Stroeken, J. H. M. (1999) "Informationtechnology and innovation in small and medium sized enterprises", Technological Forecasting and Social Change, Vol.60, No.2.

- Diniz, E. H.; Rodriguez, C. L.; Ferrer, F. (2007) "Influência governamental e estratégias institucionais na difusão de inovações em economias emergentes", RAE - revista de Administração de Empresas, Vol. 47-1, No. 1, pp 10-21.

- Donovan, J. J. (1988) "Beyond Chief Information Officer To NetWork Manager", Harvard Business Review, Vol.66, No. 5, pp134-140.

- European Commission (2003) "The new SME definition: User guide and model declaration", Official Journal of the European Union, L 124, pp. 36.

- Fávero, L. P.; Belfiore, P.; da Silva, F. L.; Chan, B. L. (2009) "Data Analysis - Multivariate Modelling for

Decision Making, Elsevier, Rio de Janeiro.

- Ferreira, F. C. M.; Goldszmidt, R. G. B.; Csillag, J. M. (2010) "The Regional Concentration of Industries and the Performance of Firms: a Multilevel Approach", BAR - Brazilian Administration Review, Vol. 7, pp. 345-361.

- Flyvbjerg, B.; Budzier, A. (2011) "Why Your IT Project May be Riskier Than You Think", Harvard Business Review, Vol. 89, No. 9, pp. 23-25.

- Gartner, Inc (2015). "Magic Quadrant for Integrated IT Portfolio Analysis Applications", Accessed on 28 Dec 2015 at http://www.gartner.com/document/3173135?ref=solrResearch&refval=160740200&qid=

- Glick, W. H.; Washburn, N. T.; Miller, C. C. (2005) "The Myth of Firm Performance", Meeting of the Academy of Management, Honolulu.

- Gomez, R.; Pather, S. (2012) "ICT Evaluation: Are We Asking the Right Questions?", The Electronic Journal on Information Systems in Developing Countries, Vol.50, No. 5, pp 1-14.

- Gonçalves, J. E. L. (1994) "Os impactos das novas tecnologias nas empresas prestadoras de serviço", RAE - Revista Administração de Empresas, Vol. 34, No.1.

- Gordon, R. J. (2001) "Technology and economic performance in the American economy", Version of paper prepared for the council on foreign relations. Forthcoming NBER Working paper.

- Govindarajan, V.; Trimble, C. O. (2011) "The CEO's Role in Business Model Reinvention", Harvard Business Review, Vol. 89, No.1, pp. 108-114.

- Groves, R. M.; Fowler Jr, F. J.; Couper, M. P.; Lepkowski, J. M.; Singer, E.; Tourangeau, R. (2004) "Survey Methodology". John Wiley.

- Hair, J.F.; Black, W.C.; Babin, B.J.; Anderson, R.E. (2010) "Multivariate Data Analysis", Prentice Hall, New Jersey.

- Hair, J.F.; Celsi, M. W.; Money, A. H.; Samouel, P.; Page, M. J. (2011) "Essentials of Business Research Methods", M. E. Sharpe, London.

- Hamel, G.; Prahalad, C. K. (1996) "Competing for the Future". Rio de Janeiro: Campus.

- Haug, A.; Pedersen, S.; Arlbjom, J. (2011) "IT readiness in small and medium-sized enterprises", Industrial Management & Data Systems, Vol. 111, No. 4, pp. 490-508.

- Henderson, J.C.; Venkatraman, N. (1993) "Strategic Alignment: Leveraging Information Technology For Transforming Organisations", IBM Systems Journal, Vol. 32, No. 1, pp4-16.

- Higon, D. A. (2011) "The impact of ICT on innovation activities: evidence for UK SMEs", International Small Business Journal, Vol. 30, No. 6, pp. 684-699.

- Hitt, L. M.; Brynjolfsson, E. (1996) "Productivity, Business Profitability, and Consumer Surplus: Three Different Measures of Information Technology Value", MIS Quarterly, Vol. 20, No. 2, pp. 121-142.

- Jeffrey, M.; Leliveld, I. (2004) "Best practices in IT portfolio management", MIT Sloan Management Review, Spring, pp. 41-49.

- Johnston, D. A.; Wade, M.; McClean R. (2007) "Does e-Business matter to SMEs? A comparison of the financial impacts of Internet Business Solutions on European and North American SMEs", Journal of Small Business Management, Vol. 45, No.3, pp. 354-361.

- Keen, P. G. W. (1993) "Information Technology and the Management Theory: The Fusion Map", IBM Systems Journal, Vol. 32, No. 1.

- Kohli, R.; Devaraj, S. (2003) "Measuring information technology payoff: a meta analysis of structural variables in firm-level empirical research", Information Systems Research, Vol. 14, No. 2, pp. 127-146.

- Kohli, R.; Grover, V. (2008) "Business Value of IT: An Essay on Expanding Research Directions to Keep Up with the Times", Journal of the Association for Information Systems, Vol. 9, n.1, p. 23-39.

- Laudon, K. C.; Laudon, J. P. (2013) "Management Information Systems", Pearson Brasil, São Paulo.

- Lefebvre, L. A.; Mason, R.; Lefebvre, E. (1997) "The Iníluence Prism in SMEs: The Power of CEO's Perceptions on Technology Policy and Its Organisational Impacts", Management Science, Vol. 43, No. 6.

- Lemos, P. M.; Pinto, F. R. T.; Zotes, L. P.; Fridman, S. (2011) "Gestão Estratégica de Empresas". São Paulo: FGV.

- Lichtenberg, F. R. (1995) "The Output Contributions of Computer Equipment and Personal: A Firm-Level Analysis", Economics of Innovation and New Technology, Vol. 3, pp. 201-217.

- Lin, B. (2007) "Information technology capability and value creation: Evidence from the US banking industry", Technology in Society, Vol. 29, pp 93-106.

- Loeser, F.; Erek, K.; Zamekow, R. (2102) "Towards a Typology of Green IS Strategies: Insights from Case Study Research", Thirty Third International Conference on Information Systems, Orlando.

- Longo, L.; Meirelles, F. S. (2015) "Impact of Investments in Information Technology on the Financial Performance of Brazilian Industries", Revista Eletrónica de Administração, v. 12, p. 1.

- Lozinsky, S. (2008) "Outsourcing as a business model: the roles and responsibilities of the company and the service provider", described in a chapter of the book "IT Outsourcing - Impacts, dilemmas, discussions and real cases", organised by Albertin, A. L. and Sanchez, O. P., Rio de Janeiro: FGV.

- Lucas, H. Jr. (1999) "Information technology and the productivity paradox: assessing the value of investing in IT", New York Oxford, Oxford University Press.

- Lucchetti, R.; Sterlacchini, A. (2004) "The adoption of ICT among SMEs: evidence from an Italian survey", Small Business Economics, Vol. 23, No. 2, pp. 151-68.

- Luftman, J. N.; Brier, T. (1999) "Achieving and Sustaining Business-IT Alignment", California Management Review, Vol. 42, No. 1.

- Luftman, J. N.; Lewis, P. R.; Oldach, S. H. (1993) "Transforming The Enterprise: The Alignment Of Business And Information Technology Strategies", IBM Systems Journal, Vol.32, No. 1, pp198-221.

- Lunardi, G. L.; Becker, J. L.; Maçada, A. C. G. (2012) "An empirical study of the impact of IT governance on organisational performance", Production, Vol. 22, No. 3, pp. 612-624.

- Lunardi, G. L.; Dolci, P. C.; Maçada, A. C. G. (2010) "Adoption of information technology and its impact on organisational performance: a study of micro and small companies", Revista de Administração, São Paulo, Vol. 45, No. 1, pp 05-17.

- Maçada, A. C. G.; Becker, J. L.; Lunardi, G. L. (2005) "Effectiveness of Conversion of IT Investments in the Efficiency of Brazilian Banks", Revista de Administração Contemporânea, Vol. 9, No. 1, pp. 9-33.

- Magutu, P. O.; Muganda, N. O.; Ondimu, G. M. (2011) "The Facets and Economic benefits of the Information Communications Technology and Innovations used by Commercial Banks in Kenya", Problems of Management in the 21st[st] Century, Vol. 2, pp. 121-140.

- Mahmood, M.A. (1993) "Associating organisational strategic performance with information technology investment: an exploratory research", European Journal of Information Systems, Vol. 2, No. 3, pp185-200.

- Maldonado, G. G.; Martínez, M. C. S.; García, D. P. L.; Aguilera, L. E.; González, M. A. (2010) "La influencia de las TICs en el rendimiento de la PyME de Aguascalientes", Investigación y Ciencia, Vol. 18(47), pp. 57-65.

- March, J. G.; Sutton, R. I. (1997) "Organisational Performance as a Dependent Variable", Organisation Science, Vol. 8, No. 6.

- Mata, F. J.; Fuerst, W. L.; Bamey, J. B. (1995) "Information Technology and Sustained Competitive Advantage: A Resource-Based Analysis", MIS Quarterly, Vol. 19, No. 4.

- McAfee, A.; Brynjolfsson, E. (2008) "Investing in IT that Makes a Competitive Difference", Harvard Business Review, Vol. 86-7, pp 98-107.

- McFarlan, W.F. (1984) "Information Technology Changes The Way You Compete", Harvard Business Review, Vol. 62, No. 3, pp98-103.

- McKeen, J. D.; Smith, H.; Parent, M. (1999) "An integrative research approach to assess the business value of Information technology", In: Mahmood, M.A. and Szewcak, E.J. Mensuring Information Technology Investment Payoff: Contemporary Approaches. Idea Group Publishing, Hershey, USA.

- Meirelles, F. (2015) "Research: IT Resource Management - Information Technology". EAESP Centre for Applied Information Technology - GVCia, São Paulo.

- Melville, N.; Gurbaxani, V.; Kraemer, K. (2007) "The productivity impact of information technology across competitive regimes: the role of industry concentration and dynamism", Decision Support Systems, Vol. 43(1), pp. 229-242.

- Melville, N.; Kraemer, K.; Gurbaxani, V. (2004) "Review: Information Technology and Organisational Performance: An Integrative Model of IT Business Value", MIS Quarterly, Vol. 28, No. 2, pp 283-322.

- Mithas, S.; Ramasubbu, N.; Sambamurthy, V. (2011) "How information management capability influences firm performance", MIS Quarterly, Vol. 35, No. 1, pp. 237-256.

- Mithas, S.; Tafti, A.; Bardhan, I.; Goh, J. M. (2012) "Information Technology and Firm Profitability: Mechanisms and Empirical Evidence", MIS Quarterly, Vol. 36, No. 1, pp. 205224.

- Moore, G. C.; Benbasat, I. (1991) "Development of an Instrument to Measure the Perceptions of Adopting an Information Technology Innovation", Information Systems Research, Vol. 2, No. 3.

- Mooney, J. G.; Gurbaxani, V.; Kraemer, K. L. (1996) "A Process Oriented Framework for Assessing the Business Value of Information Technology", The Data Base for Advances in Information Systems, Vol.

27, No. 2.

- Moraes, G. H. S. M.; Cappellozza, A.; Meirelles, F. S. (2011) "Is it the end of paper? Technological Advances and Their Possible Impacts on Paper Consumption", Intemext - Electronic Journal of International Business at ESPM, Vol. 6, pp.48-65.

- Mustafa, H. H. (2015) "The Role of ICT Management to Achieve Organisational Innovation", The International Journal of Organisational Innovation, Vol. 7, No. 4.

- Nakata, C.; Zhu, Z.; Kraimer, M. L. (2008) "The complex contribution of Information technology capability to business performance", Journal of Managerial Issues, pp. 485-506.

- Neely, A.; Gregory, M.; Platts, K. (2005) "Performance measurement system design - A literature review and research agenda", International Journal of Operations & Production Management, Vol. 25, No. 12, pp 1228-1263.

- Nevo, S.; Wade, M.; Cook, W. (2010) "An empirical study of IT as a factor of production: the case of net-enabled IT assets", Information Systems Frontiers, Vol. 12, No. 3, pp.323-335.

- Nolan, R. L. (1979) "Managing the Crises in Data Processing", Harvard Business Review, Vol.57, No. 2, pp115-126.

- Nolan, R.; McFarlan, F. W. (2005) "Information Technology and the Board of Directors", Harvard Business review, Vol. 83, No. 10, pp 96-106.

- Ollo-López, A.; Aramendía-Muneta, M. E. (2012) "ICT impact on competitiveness, innovation and enviroment", Telematics and Informatics, Vol. 29, pp204-210.

- Orlikowski, W. J. (2000) "Using Technology and Constituting Structures: A Practice Lens for Studying Technology in Organisations", Organisation Science, Vol. 11, No. 42.

- Orlikowski, W. J.; Baroudi, J. J. (1991) "Studying Information Technology in Organisations: research Approaches and Assumptions", Information Systems Research, Vol. 2, No. 1.

- Otim, S.; Dow, K. E.; Grove, V.; Wong, J. A. (2012) "The Impact of Information Technology Investments on Downside Risk of the Firm: Alternative Measurement of the Business Value of IT", Journal of Management Information Systems, Vol. 29, No. 1, pp. 159-193.

- Ouakouak, M. L.; Ouedraogo, N. (2013) "The mediating role of employee strategic alignment in the relationship between rational strategic planning and firm performance: a European study", Canadian

Journal of Administrative Sciences, Vol.30, pp.143-158.

- Parker, C. M.; Castleman, T. (2007) "New directions for research on SME-eBusiness: insights from an analysis of joumal articles from 2003 to 2006", Journal of Information Systems and Small Business, Vol. 1, No. 1-2, pp21-40.

- Pérez, R.; Garzón, M.; Nieto, M. (2009) "Empirical analysis of the application of the management modelling model for organisations in Colombian SMEs", Revista EAN, Vol. 65, pp. 77-105.

- Piccoli, G.; Ives, B. (2005) "Review: IT-Dependent Strategic Initiatives and Sustained Competitive Advantage: A Review and Synthesis of The Literature", MIS Quarterly, Vol. 29, No. 4, pp 747-776.

- Piget, P.; Kossai, M. (2013) "The Relationship between Information and Communication Technology Use and Firm Performance in Developing Countries: A Case Study of Electrical and Electronic Goods Manufacturing SMEs in Tunisia", African Development Review, Vol. 25, No. 3, pp. 330-343.

- Prates, G. A.; Ospina, M. T. (2004) "Information Technology in Small Businesses: Success Factors, Restrictions and Benefits", RAC - Revista de Administração Contemporânea, Vol. 8, No. 2, pp 9-26.

- Ravichandran, T.; Liu, Y.; Han, S.; Hasan, I. (2009) "Diversification and Firm Performance: Exploring the Moderating Effects of Information Technology Spending", Journal of Management Information Systems, Vol. 25, No. 4, pp 205-240.

- Rajanen, D.; Salminen, M.; Ravaja, N. (2015) "Psychophysiological Responses to Digital Media: Frontal EEG Alpha Asymmetry during Newspaper Reading on a Tablet versus Print", Academic Mindtrek 15, Finland.

- Remenyi, D. (2000) "The elusive nature of delivering benefits from IT investment", Electronic Journal of Information Systems Evaluation, Vol. 3, No. 1.

- Remenyi, D.; Griffiths, P. D. R.; Diniz, E. H. (2004) "The manager in the field and Information and Communications Technology success", Proceedings of the 11 th European Conference on Information Technology Evaluation, pp. 359-370, Amsterdam.

- Riascos, S. C.; Aguilera, A. (2011) " Herramientas TIC como apoyo a la gestión del talento humano", Cuademos de Administración, Vol. 27(46), pp. 141-154.

- Romesburg, H. C. (1990) "Cluster Analysis for Researchers", Krieger Publishing Company, Malabar, Florida.

- SEBRAE - Brazilian Micro and Small Business Support Service (2014) "Entrepreneurship in Brazil", Global Entrepreneurship Monitor - GEM.

- Sekaran, U. (2000) "Research methods for business: a skill-building approach", 3rd ed.

- Sharma, S. (1996) "Applied Multivariate Techniques", John Wiley & Sons, New York.

- Sicsú, A. L. (1996) "Cluster Analysis", Didactic Texts Series, EAESP, FGV-SP.

- Seddon, P. B.; Calvert, C.; Yang, S. (2010) "A multi-project model of key factors affecting organisational benefits from enterprise systems", MIS Quarterly, Vol. 34, No. 2, pp. 305-328.

- Southern, A.; Tilley, F. (2000) "Small firms and information and communication technologies (ICTs): towards a typology of ICTs usage", New Technology, Work and Employment, Vol. 15, No. 2, pp 138-154.

- Stang, D. C.; Duggan, J. (2015) "Magic Quadrant for Integrated IT Portfolio Analysis Applications", Gartner, G00272277.

- Stanworth, C. (1998) "Telework and the information age", New Technology, Work and Employment, Vol. 13, No. 1.

- Steinfield, C.; LaRose, R.; Chew, H. E.; Tong, S. T. (2012) "Small and medium-sized enterprises in rural business clusters: the relation between ICT adoption and benefits derived from cluster membership", The Information Society, Vol. 28, pp. 110-120.

- Tallon, P.; Kraemer, K. (2007) "Fact or Fiction? A sensemaking perspective on the reality behind executive perceptions of IT business value", Journal of Management Information Systems, Vol. 24, No. 1, pp13-54.

- Triplett, J. E. (1999) "The Slow Productivity Paradox: What do computers do to productivity?", The Canadian Journal of Economics, Special Issue on Service Sector Productivity and the Productivity Paradox, Vol. 32(2), pp.309-334.

- Venkatraman, N.; Ramanujam, V. (1986) "Measurement of Business Performance in Strategy Research: A Comparison of Approaches", Academy of Management Review, Vol. 11, No. 4, pp 801-814.

- Weill, P. (1992) "The Relationship between Investment in Information Technology and Firm Performance: A Study of the Valve Manufacturing Sector", Information Systems Research, Vol. 3, No. 4.

- Weill, P. (2006) "Generating Premium Returns on Your IT Investments", MIT Sloan Management Review,

Vol. 47, No. 2, pp. 39-48.

- Weill, P.; Broadbent, M. (1998) "Leavering the new infrastructure: how market leaders capitalise on IT", Boston: Harvard Business School Press.

- Weill, P.; Ross, J. W. (2004) "IT Governance: how top performers manage IT decision rights for superior results", Boston: Harvard Business School Press.

- Weill, P.; Ross, J. W. (2006) "IT Governance - Information Technology", Editora M. Books, São Paulo.

- Weill, P.; Woerner, S. L.; Mocker, M. (2014) "How Top Performers Manage Total Digitisation", MIT CISR Research Briefmg, Vol. 14, No. 4.

- Wernerfelt, B.; Montgomery, C. A. (1988) "Tobin's q and the Importance of Focus in Firm Performance", The American Economic Review, Vol. 78, No. 1, pp. 246-250.

- Wolff, E. N. (1999) "The productivity Paradox: Evidence from indirect indicators of Service sector productivity growth", The Canadian Journal of Economics, Vol. 32(2), Special Issue on Service Sector Productivity Paradox, pp. 231-308.

- Wu, M.; Lee, T.; Tsai, T.; Huang, C.; Wu, F. F.; Mills, M. E. (2015) "Evaluation of a Mobile Station Electronic Health Record on Documentation Compliance and Nurses' Attitudes", Open Journal of Nursing, Vol. 5, pp. 678-688.

- Yen-Tsang, C.; Csillag, J. M.; Siegler, J. (2012) "Theory of Reasoned Action for continuous improvement capabilities: a behavioural approach", RAE - Revista de Administração de Empresas, Vol. 52, No. 5, pp. 546-564.

- Yoo, Y (2010) "Computing in Everyday Life - A Call for Research on Experiential Computing", MIS Quarterly, Vol. 34, No. 2, pp. 213-231.

Appendix A - Pilot questionnaire

<table>
<tr><td colspan="5">Company name</td><td colspan="5">CNPJ</td></tr>
<tr><td>Address</td><td colspan="9"></td></tr>
<tr><td>City</td><td></td><td>State</td><td></td><td>POST COD E</td><td></td><td>Phone</td><td colspan="3"></td></tr>
<tr><td colspan="3">Sector (Industry/Trade/Services/Public Services)</td><td colspan="2"></td><td>Branch</td><td colspan="4"></td></tr>
<tr><td colspan="2">Responsible for the information</td><td colspan="8"></td></tr>
<tr><td colspan="3">Position</td><td colspan="2">E-Mail</td><td colspan="5"></td></tr>
<tr><td colspan="5"></td><td>2010</td><td>2011</td><td>2012</td><td>2013</td><td>2014</td></tr>
<tr><td colspan="5">Total Number of Company Employees</td><td></td><td></td><td></td><td></td><td></td></tr>
<tr><td colspan="5">Net Annual Revenue (approx. in thousand reais)</td><td></td><td></td><td></td><td></td><td></td></tr>
</table>

Annual Net Profit (approx. in thousand reais)					
Total IT expenditure *(including third parties) = Personnel+Expenses+Investments*					
Total number of company devices: "Keyboards in use" (owners)					
In what year did your company start using IT, for example for financial management, tax control, payroll, accounting, stock control or any other application?					
	I totally agree	Partially agree	Indifferent	Partially disagree	I totally disagree
Computerisation has had an effect on your company's management					
Do you believe that this process has had an effect on the following aspects?					
Operational efficiency					
More effective customer relations					
Smarter decision-making					
Innovation and business transformation					
IT in your company has a strategic impact on the following aspects:					
Operational efficiency					
More effective customer relations					
Smarter decision-making					
Innovation and business transformation					
In the future, IT will play a strategic role in your company in the following aspects:					
Operational efficiency					
More effective customer relations					
Smarter decision-making					
Innovation and business transformation					
The use of IT should revolutionise your company's business model within a maximum of 3 years					
The use of IT should revolutionise your company's business model within a maximum of 6 years					
The recent legal changes obliging companies to submit their tax obligations digitally have had an impact on hiring more IT applications and forced your company to invest more in IT.					

Appendix B - Final questionnaire used for data collection

Company name		**CNPJ**	
Address			
City	**State**	**POSTCODE**	**Phone**
Sector (Industry/Trade/Services/Public Services) Industry			
Responsible for the information			
Job title E-Mail			

	2012	**2013**	**2014**
Total Number of Company Employees			
Net Annual Revenue (approx. in thousand reais)			
Annual Net Profit (approx. in thousand reais)			
Total IT expenditure *(including third parties) = Personnel+Expenses+Investments*			
Total Number of Company Devices: "Keyboards in use" (owners) (desktops + notebooks + tablets)			
What year did your company start using IT?			

	I totally agree	Partially agree	Partially disagree	Strongly disagree

Today, IT in your company contributes to				
Cost reduction				
Increased productivity				
New products and/or services				
In the future, IT will contribute to your company:				
Cost reduction				
Increased productivity				
New products and/or services				
The use of IT will change the way your company operates in the market in no more than 5 years.				
The legal changes requiring companies to submit their tax obligations digitally have had an impact on the hiring of more tax applications. **IT and forced your company to invest more in IT**				

MIX
Papier aus verantwortungsvollen Quellen
Paper from responsible sources
FSC® C105338

Printed by Books on Demand GmbH, Norderstedt / Germany